THE
INCOMPLEAT
ANGLER

THE
INCOMPLEAT
ANGLER

A Fly Fishing
Odyssey

by
Jim Enger

Foreword by Ted Williams
Illustrations by Chuck Forman

Countrysport Press
New Albany, Ohio

Five of the stories in this book first appeared in *Fly Rod & Reel*: "Getting Out of Dodge," "The Guide As...," "The Master of Frenchman's Pond—Robert Traver," "The True Story of the Dancing Fly and Other Notes From Frenchman's Pond," and "The Gurgle of Great Expectations."

This edition of *The Incompleat Angler* was printed by Jostens Book Manufacturing, State College, Pennsylvania. The book was designed by Angela Saxon of Saxon Design, Traverse City, Michigan. The text is set in Apollo.

© 1996 by Jim Enger
Illustrations © 1996 by Chuck Forman

First Edition
10 9 8 7 6 5 4 3 2 1

Published by Countrysport Press
15 South High Street, New Albany, Ohio 43054-0166

Printed in the United States of America

ISBN 0-924357-59-2 (trade ed.)
ISBN 0-924357-60-6 (limited ed.)

Library of Congress Cataloging-in-Publication Data

Enger, Jim, 1946–
    The incompleat angler : a fly fishing odyssey / by Jim Enger.
        p.   cm.
        1. Fly fishing—Anecdotes. 2. Enger, Jim, 1946– . I. Title.
SH 456.E54 1996
    799.1'2—dc20   96-7082
                                                                 CIP

To Pete Treboldi

CONTENTS

❖

FOREWORD

Jim Enger has had the same eroding influence on one of my pet theories that his fishing buddy Pete had on the dish of peas he fell asleep in and snored all over the table as if they were green hail stones bouncing across a parking lot. That theory is that hook-and-bullet journalism is an oxymoron. Every time I pick up something by Enger he reminds me that my theory has a few holes in it.

He is, to borrow Tom McGuane's memorable phrase, "a man ruined by sport." But only financially, because it is sport or at least, as Enger says, "where you end up doing it," that has imbued him with the ability to perceive what's important. He reports what he feels when he participates in the earth as man did not make it. He has the eye of a northern harrier, the ear of a whitetail. No shred of beauty, irony, or humor escapes him. Like his friend and mentor, the late John Voelker, he writes with impiety and honesty. Like Voelker, he is a chronicler of magic and madness.

Unlike the outdoor typists on whom I base my theory, Enger did not learn what he knows from a guide named Jim. He is the guide named Jim. He is not interested in churning out "how-to-do-it" pieces; and he is not willing to churn out "where-to-go" pieces, having been schooled by the sly, artful

Voelker in the precaution and good form of sweeping away one's spoor and never tattling on trout one has dallied with.

"All 'news,' as it is called, is gossip," wrote Thoreau. "And they who read and edit it are old women over their tea." But Enger reports genuine news—the sounds, scents, sights, feelings, and happenings of the real world, a world unmolested by humanity, a world hostile to all but the humble. "News," as Enger calls it, has never occurred in Detroit and only once in Chicago (when Mrs. O'Leary's cow conducted habitat restoration). It happens most in low, wet, wild places—the clatter of hummingbird-sized hexes, for instance; a beaver dam so fresh as to be muckless; the yodeling of the magnificent eastern canids we wrongly call coyotes; goose music drifting down through still afternoons; golden tamaracks reflected up from troutwater; whisker moons etched on azure, chamber-of-commerce sunsets splashed across northern skies; a puppy point on wild turkeys; the sweet-sour scent of grouse woods; the heady fragrance of balsam and bog mud; the caroling of whitethroats and whippoor-wills; the pulse of a stream-bred trout transferred through a wisp of graphite, into your wrist, brain, heart, and soul. In short, Enger reports on everything that bores the editors of big outdoor magazines (the only kind that pay you more than it costs to research the story).

The editors, in turn, are obsessed with everything that bores Enger—mostly gadgets. As another of my favorite outdoor writers once put it, "I have the impression that the American sportsman is puzzled; he doesn't understand what is happening to him. Bigger and better gadgets are good for industry, so why not for outdoor recreation? It has not dawned on him that outdoor recreations are essentially primitive, atavistic; that their value is contrast-value; that excessive mechanization destroys contrasts by moving the factory to the woods or to the marsh. The sportsman has no leaders to tell him what is wrong. The sporting press no longer represents sport; it has turned billboard for the gadgeteer." This writer was Aldo Leopold, circa 1948.

I scarcely dare imagine what he would write today were he forced to listen to boom boxes amidst a tin-boat hatch, or were he transported to a BASS Masters Classic—" the test of the best"—where commercial barkers peddle hi-tech gadgetry as if it were Dr. Kickapoo's Elixir for Rheum, Ague, Blindness, and Insanity.

Did Enger acquire his values and tastes from Voelker or did he seek Voelker out because he already had them? Probably both, but more the latter. Me too, I think. Voelker believed that you could tell a lot about a man by the way he handled a fly rod. From the church pew on the chipmunk bridge (the one with some ancient sinner's gum stuck underneath) he scrutinized the loops I threw to his troutlings; and no compliment I ever received gave me a bigger rush than his endorsement of my eccentric side-arm style. I, in turn, assessed Voelker—or, rather, confirmed past assessments—not by how he handled his rod but by the rod itself. Doubtless, it still hangs on the wall of the old cabin, because none of his friends would use such a buggy whip and not even the most desperate of U.P. thieves would deign to steal it. It was his "camp rod," the only one of dozens he owned that he dared leave at Frenchman's Pond. The reel was plastic; the rod black, tinsel-wrapped fiberglass—the kind of outfit you pick up at the supermarket for $29.99. He used it often. Such was our professor's devotion to gadgets.

"What a coincidence," I would always exclaim to myself on perceiving from Enger's copy how he got things exactly "right," and how the rambling worm trails of our lives kept intersecting. But now that I've digested these stunning stories, I understand what should have been obvious to me. None of it has been a coincidence. Of course we carouse in the same whiskey-soaked, cigar-stained circles. Where else would we be considered socially acceptable? Of course we would independently seek out Voelker in the hangover of our youth. Who else could teach us the roll casts of good living and good writing? Of course we would work mostly for small hook-and-bullet magazines, the only ones not run by their ad departments. Where else can you say anything important about fishing and hunting? Of course we would find Silvio Calabi at *Fly Rod & Reel*. Who else wouldn't be shocked and repulsed by our best work?

Enger still had his downstate fly shop when he presented John Voelker with a spool of 7X tippet material. In September 1980, when I at last made it out to Frenchman's, Enger had just put him onto 10X. There was the sage of the U.P., sitting on his cabin steps, perusing a letter from a friend who had compared tying on 10X to "catching a fart in the wind." Voelker read the simile aloud, nodding approvingly. "Not bad," he intoned. "Not bad at all." Maybe it was Enger who wrote that; it has his signature all over it. In any case, he's always getting away with that kind of stuff at *Fly Rod & Reel*. But try to imagine reading it on the pious pages of some of the bigger outdoor magazines.

I see Voelker in Enger's writing all the time, and maybe Enger sees him in mine. Something as simple as our overuse of the word "doubtless," for instance. Most copy editors, who are usually under thirty and named "Muffy" and "Bubbles," never miss a chance to change "doubtless" to "doubtlessly." It was, after all, Muffy and Bubbles who taught me what I call the First Maxim of Journalism, i.e., that no hectic raging in our species' blood—not discounting thirst, hunger, substance addiction, and sexual lust—is more compelling than the urge of one human being to change the written words of another. But God help the human being who attempted such vandalism on the prose of Judge John Voelker. I was his editor at *Gray's Sporting Journal,* a terrifying job at first. But he taught me what he taught Enger—that words are more important than even we anal word-retainers had supposed, that there is no task more difficult than writing one graceful sentence and no task easier than ruining it.

The Jim Engers of America constitute a cultural backwater, a backwater that includes you because you've bothered to read this far, and no one reads a foreword first. Consider our aberrant reaction to eastern coyotes. For each of us who rejoices in their choruses and even their unseen, unheard presence, there are five thousand who are at least as incensed as the Michigan Legislature, and who have no doubt that when the coyotes consume all the deer they'll switch to cows, then chickens, and finally, children. It's the same everywhere—next door to me, in fact. According to the *Worcester Telegram and Gazette,* the residents of Holden, Massachusetts, who have acclimated so beautifully to the sounds of mechanized megalopolis, are outraged about the noise pollution they must endure at the throats of the local coyote pack that has taken to answering train whistles. No complaints to the press, though, about the local motorcycle pack that howls and revs (possibly in response to grinding truck gears) out there on Routes 32 and 190. Michigan pols and Holden yuppies represent normalcy in America. It is they, not us, who are in step with society. We are the misfits, the pariahs, Yeats' weird, wandering Aenguses with fire in our heads who stumble after silver trout and glimmering girls when white moths are on the wing.

I know without ever having asked that Jim Enger envies normal society its obsession with golf. The land on which one chases the little white balls is not being sold off to hack-and-gouge developers. In fact, it is being *produced* by hack-and-gouge developers. Recruitment of the little white balls themselves always outstrips the rate at which they are depleted. Dammers, gutterizers, grazers, de-waterers, and fillet-and-release pork-chop soakers cannot in concert reduce their numbers. You just chip them into the pond and buy more. All this is why the golfers I know are content, well adjusted, and noted for their lack of bile (save No-Birds Daviau, who threatens to play golf whenever the Maine brook trout aren't biting, and worries that they are biting whenever he tees off). They have adapted. We, on the other hand, have fallen with the spinners into streamside tar pits and, reels submerged in muck, are vainly groping for brittle branches with the tips of our fly rods.

Because our society sets such a low priority on wild things and wild places, the few Jim Engers in our midst have collapsed into literary pulsars, emitting periodic bursts of brilliance whenever they collect enough money to afford fuel and food. During the dark phases of their rotations (unless they strike it rich, as did the master with *Anatomy of a Murder,* a work inferior to *Anatomy of a Fisherman* and most of the other rare books he authored) they must write about subjects like shipping pallets, car wax, conveyors, spark plugs, light bulbs, and lubricants (not even the kind you drink). This is the way of our culture.

So it was utterly inevitable that I should fish with Enger in his twenty-inch-brook-trout bog on the evening of the day I met him, with Hexes buzzing all around us and his beloved yodel dogs at full cry. The music was just as he describes: "There were puppies in both groups, and the combination of serious, adult wailing and the comical breaking voices of the pups created a festive atmosphere." It was wonderful, just like one of his stories.

In a century or two Jim Enger will be plucked from his tar pit and studied. Meanwhile, pay attention to this collection. Savor it. Share it. It is outdoor literature, and it will last.

Ted Williams
Grafton, Massachusetts

PREFACE

One summer in the 1950s my uncle, Pat Holland, took me fishing for the first time in my life in a small, muddy creek in the mountains of West Virginia. I caught a bass about ten inches long and poison ivy that covered me from head to toe. One itch started the next day, but another itch started the moment that little largemouth gut-hooked itself on that night crawler. I was gut-hooked too.

I had to show the fish to everyone, and finally that evening my grandfather cleaned it. "We'll do it in the garage while I visit with my friend Jim Beam," he whispered. I didn't make the connection with the bottle he had hidden behind his workbench and wondered why Mr. Beam hadn't stopped by.

My mother's father, who was something of a wildcat, lived in a big house that overlooked the Ohio River, wore white linen suits, and was always on the outs with my father and uncle. But Granddaddy Crockett and I were pretty thick. I was the first-born grandchild in what turned out to be a rather large family when you counted all my cousins, and he doted on me. He bought me my first pocketknife and would take me with him when he went for "vegetables." On our rare visits, he'd let me sit on his lap and steer the big Buick he drove. The vegetable run usually included some mischief involving various beverages. One vegetable outing turned into an all-afternoon affair where the beverage of choice was clear and came in a quart jar from a shack back in the holler. Arriving back at the house, reeking of 'shine, Granddaddy caught hell from my mother and step-grandmother.

But that night, in his garage, he cleaned that bass in an operation that lasted nearly an hour, maybe more. Actually, it was more like a dissection. I didn't realize until much later that the length of time it took to fillet that bass allowed a fair amount of interplay with the bottle so craftily tucked away behind the workbench. Then, too, he was playing to a fascinated audience, and he knew it.

Like most little kids, I had a morbid sense of curiosity. I was a rapt student as I watched that little bass come apart on the workbench. The last thing he did was to open the stomach, which he had earlier laid on the newspaper. Out came a partially digested crawfish and I was amazed. At that moment, on that steamy West Virginia evening, with hundreds of fireflies sparkling on my grandfather's broad, sloping lawn, I began to sense that there was a connection between things. I knew what crawfish were; I had caught them in my northern Ohio creeks. I liked to see them raise their tiny pincers when I cornered one, a one-ounce bit of nothing rising in defiance to an agitator thousands of times its size.

So that was the day, on Twelve Pole Creek with my uncle, that I ran afoul of two types of itches. One would make me miserable for a couple of weeks. The other has dogged me all my life. With that small bass, I connected with something out of another world, a liquid universe full of mystery, a watery cosmos full of secrets—and I wanted to know them all.

I went through all the stages: carp and bullhead from discolored creeks; bluegills and sunfish from farm ponds; pike and bass from old gravel pits; perch and white bass from Lake Erie. Throughout it all, one thing remained constant: There was always something to learn. Once, on the pier behind the local power company's Lake Erie plant, dozens of fishermen all around me caught white bass on every cast while I caught none. Finally one old fart said, "You're rigged up wrong, kid," as he walked away with a bucket full of wriggling white bass. (To get to that pier, which was posted and off-limits, you had to scale an eight-foot Cyclone fence. When the white bass were running, everyone ignored the "Keep Out—Danger" signs, and it looked like a massive prison break, half of it in reverse, as pier-bound anglers climbed one way and anglers who had limited-out climbed the other way. Knowing they were vastly outnumbered, the power company guards ignored the whole thing.) Eventually, of course, I learned how to rig up for white bass and caught my share. That was about the time I started to think I had a handle on this fishing thing. And then, a year after I graduated from high school, we moved to Michigan and I discovered trout. And fly fishing. And everything went to hell.

In his book, *Trout from the Hills,* Ian Niall wrote: "There is no such thing as a book of rules, written or unwritten, on the art of catching a trout with a fly. A master can fail, a novice can be blessed. If a man lives all his time he will learn the ways of trout. He will also learn humility."

Amen, brother Niall. Humility is the operative word. I'm not sure that if I stick around for a few more decades I'll learn the ways of trout. I'm working on it. But I've sure been humiliated enough times.

So far, the only thing I've learned about trout fishing I learned back in those panfish days. Sort of like the guy who said everything he needed to know about life he learned in kindergarten. In trout fishing, as in everything that involves nature, there is no such thing as a sure thing. Which is one of the things that fascinates me about this game. God help us if the techniques, tips, and advice offered in the avalanche of books and videos arriving daily work every time. With all the pieces of the puzzle in place there wouldn't be any mystery.

But maybe someone will figure out how to catch a trout every time they go trout fishing. There seems to be no shortage of people working on it. Who knows? Maybe it will be me. But I doubt it. Every time I think I've got it wired, I discover some puzzle, some little mystery that needs to be solved. Some I get, some I don't. Which is why I remain, happily, an incompleat angler.

Jim Enger
Au Sable River

ACKNOWLEDGMENTS

Along the way some special fishermen have touched my life: My son, Jeff; Pete Treboldi, my fishing partner for twenty-five years; Rob "The Maz" Mazzeo, accomplice on many a misadventure; John Sligay; the late John Voelker (aka Robert Traver), mentor and friend for nearly twenty years; my brother-in-law, Ron "Olive Matuka" Randlett; Lou and Tom Black; John Barton; Greg Gerling; Doc Elliott; Carol Walkon; Paul Bleichner; Paul Lienert; Rusty Gates; Craig Perry; Charlie Weaver; Ed McGlinn; Jeff Gardner; Dan Alstott; Ted Bogdan; Pat Dwyer; Chuck Forman; the late Craig Woods, colleague and beloved co-conspirator; my late father, R. J. "Dick" Enger, who "discovered" the Au Sable River for us; and especially my uncle, Robert Patrick Holland, who first took me fishing in a muddy Appalachian creek called Twelve Pole.

I must also thank three other people who have touched my life in a special way: my wife, Diana Saillant-Enger (pronounced "Deanna" in the Spanish of her native Dominican Republic), who always has the ready smile and never complains when the Big White Bear lights out again to some distant stream in search of that perfect pool; and the two beautiful princesses, my daughters Sally and Christine.

And a special thanks to Doug Truax, who was instrumental in getting this project off the ground, and to Art DeLaurier Jr., whose editing touch was delicate and precise.

The author would also like to thank Judith Martin, aka Miss Manners, for her contribution to Chapter 3.

Lacsa Airlines, the official airline of Costa Rica, kindly provided transportation assistance.

❖

"When I was a boy…it was the custom among my people that the young men take a wild creature as their cipher, a mark of their approaching manhood, a badge of character. On a raw spring day the young men assembled by the big river that snaked across the prairie. The sun was just rising and the dawn spread across the vast plains, a land that seemed to reach beyond time itself. And we young men then chose. Fox. Panther. Eagle. Deer. Bear. Horse. When my turn arrived I said loudly, clearly, proudly, 'Trout.' My father smiled and was not ashamed. From that moment on, the trout and I have been inseparable."

—Elias Wonder (the old fly fishing Indian)
Harry Middleton
The Earth is Enough

"Women… win the final victory when they trap themselves a wild boy and turn him into a house pet. Or try to."

—The Old Man
Robert Ruark
The Old Man and the Boy

"The final question is, should any man turn his back on ambition, profit, security, and a parking place in the city, just to pursue a fish!"

—Grandfather Emerson Newell
Harry Middleton
The Earth is Enough

1

❖

GETTING OUT
OF DODGE

There I was, sitting on a hummock at dusk a few hundred yards into a northern Michigan marsh next to a sweet little creek. The creek came out of a distant cedar swamp. I had five cans of Miller Genuine Draft in the stream and one in my hand. For as far as I could see there was nothing but waist-high grass, an occasional swale of what we call tag alders, and a lone high spot of land sporting a few red pines.

We go from season to season, river to river, hatch to hatch searching for that perfect pool, and I was beginning to think I had found mine. Behind me the sun was sliding beyond the tops of the cedars, turning a line of mare's tails to an outrageous pink. I turned often to see it and I knew that others were watching too; fortunately, not where I was. All over the north—on clear lakes and rivers, from cottage porches, from atop the dunes along Lake Michigan and in the lakeside villages, from the bluffs above the old Indian town of Cross Village—the pace slows as people stop to watch the dramatically colored tendrils sweep high into the sky. The tourists enjoying dinner on the world's longest veranda at the Grand Hotel on Mackinac Island were getting their money's worth this evening.

Back in my bog the yodel dogs started to sing. There seemed to be two families of coyotes that lived and hunted in the swamp, and when one group started to sing, the other agreed that it was a fine evening for some music. There were puppies in both groups, and the combination of serious, adult wailing and the comical breaking voices of the pups created a festive atmosphere, just the right prelude to what I hoped would happen shortly in the air over the stream. Motivated perhaps by the Michigan Tourist Council sunset, the two families set up a racket. One pack seemed to be moving up the creek toward me, and I longed for a glimpse of the gang, especially the pups.

I did not see them, of course. Coyotes are extremely wary, and in addition to drinking the Miller, I was also smoking a cigar (an extremely good imported number that I had saved for a moment like this one), sending AWACS-like signals to Wile E. and his merry band.

In Michigan you mostly see them from the car as they dart across the road. They are not nearly as numerous as they are in western states and do no harm. But for years they were responsible for all sorts of witless antics on both floors of the state legislature in Lansing.

The Michigan legislature comprises politicians from one of the largest cities in the country, and politicians who represent areas so remote and wild that a very high percentage of their constituents practically live off the land. That the state is divided in half by water adds another dimension. The legislators from the top half, as well as many of the folks they represent, not so secretly believe that the Upper Peninsula is its own state every way but legally.

For years there has been a bounty on coyotes in Michigan. And each year, mostly in the U.P., several dozen are killed, their ears turned in, and the small bounty paid as prescribed by law. (Pointy-eared dogs in certain parts of the U.P. have learned to look over their shoulders.)

For reasons not entirely clear, the politicians from downstate would annually mount a big effort to get the coyote bounty repealed when the legislature reconvened and new bills were introduced. It wasn't long before Lansing-watchers began to look forward to the yearly battle between the slickers from the big city and the representatives from across the Straits of Mackinac.

The downstate politicians were never successful, despite all sorts of chicanery in the smoke-filled back rooms of Lansing. The politicos of the U.P. are elected term after term, have seniority, and chair important committees. Thus, the distinguished representative from distant Dollar Bay might suggest to the distinguished representative from Detroit that if the good citizens of the Motor City really wanted those nifty road improvements, the good citizens of Dollar Bay ought to be allowed to collect the bounty on a few ky-oat-eez.

The year the big-city mob came closest, one U.P. legislator left his hospital bed to reach the floor in time to vote, while another stood in chambers embracing a stuffed baby deer. The gentleman with the taxidermy said that every spring there were plenty of *these* (he holds stuffed fawn aloft) in his district, but if the bounty were repealed his folks would be ass-deep in coyotes. As everyone knew, he said, they bred indiscriminately. Once again, the downstaters retreated with their tails between their legs, so to speak.

❖

The sky deepened and now the fireflies were out and about. Ten yards in front of me the creek curved sharply, and within the curve there was a deep hole. What I was waiting for while sitting on the hummock and drinking beer, smoking cigars, watching sunsets and fireflies, and listening to yodel dogs, was the appearance of Mr. and Mrs. Hexagenia limbata. This little creek gets a tremendous hatch of the giant mayfly.

This is an intoxicating piece of water, and over the course of the summer I had become addicted to it. It can be fished up or down, it is wide open yet remote, and it holds browns and brookies. A friend had been nice enough to show it to me and we often fished it together sharing a rod. We discovered that this was a pleasant way to fish, both for camaraderie and convenience. We would pussyfoot from one pool to the next, exchanging the rod and advice every so many casts or after each trout. The guy who didn't have the rod carried the beer.

It was almost dark, and still the big mayflies didn't come. This isn't at all unusual for the Hex, but they had come just at dusk two evenings in a row, and I am not much of, night fisherman anymore. Over the years I have come to fish for reasons that often have little to do with catching a lot of trout or timing probable hatches to the second. The reasons have more to do with going when I'm genuinely in the mood and when I'm likely to see things. I have come to use the sport as an instrument to bring me a variety of pleasures, and a trout taking a fly is just one of them, no more or no less important than any of the others.

This has not always been the case. For a while—but not for long—the sheer number of hours spent in the river meant everything, and the only object was to catch a lot of trout. A group of us ran together and we fished very hard. When we weren't fishing we raised hell. Everything was done to excess and we were very good at it—all of it. There was nothing contemplative about those days.

I had no desire to hang around until midnight, which diehard Hex fishermen routinely do waiting for the hatch or spinner fall. I decided to give the bugs an honest hour. I was armed with beverages and smokes and the mosquitoes weren't bad.

It was then that the enormity of what I had done struck me. Here it was, the end of June, and I had not worked a single day since February. I had about sixty dollars to my name and the immediate prospects for any more dough were slim.

In February I had spent a weekend with a friend at her cabin on a river in northern Michigan. It turned out to be a watershed weekend for both of us. She decided that her marriage was worth saving and I decided that it was time to call in the dogs and piss on the fire. Twenty-two years in the advertising trenches were enough.

I called my secretary that Sunday, dictated my letter of resignation, and thus removed myself from the world of commerce. I had done this before, but always on a temporary basis. And directly or indirectly, trout and trout country were almost always responsible, much to the consternation of a variety of bosses, no less so to wives and girlfriends. But advertising types are supposed to be a touch distracted. And when the chips were really down, a decent portfolio always landed another writing job. I had written about cars, bread, car wax, plastic shipping pallets, conveyors, fishing tackle, public transportation, lubricants, marinas, beer, storage racks, robots, pest control, a restaurant, rocket engines, spark plugs, light bulbs, and quickie tune-up centers. When I made the phone call in February I had worked at the same job for nearly four years. My friends thought I had either gone straight or crazy, but they all agreed it was a miracle.

❖

Still no sex-driven Hexes, and my head was full of the past.

They want a new approach to their TV stuff, the boss was saying. I am gazing out the window. It is a Thursday evening and I can see it coming. I was scheduled to be off the next day. It was May and there was a sparkling little meadow stretch of the Boardman I wanted to fish. I wanted three uninterrupted days in the sunshine 250 miles north to fish Pale Morning Duns and #16 Adamses to the gorgeous little browns and brookies that lay in ambush there. I wanted to sit in the greening meadow and drink brandy from my flask and write letters to the woman I loved. I had a momentary vision, imagining her next to me in the meadow, her raven hair flashing in the sunlight. But the boss is saying that he has made arrangements for me to ride with a bread truck driver. From my eleventh floor window I can see a hawk circling a suburban neighborhood. The boss is saying that if I ride one of the bread trucks maybe I'll get some new angle we can use for TV spots. Be at the bakery at 2:30 in the morning.

I spend half the night riding a bread truck. Not only don't I get inspired, but I get hot and sweaty because I end up helping the driver, who is overjoyed at having company. I see the inside of more grocery stores in eight hours than I expected to see in my lifetime. We get back to the bakery and I am tired and angry. I notice two women in the mailroom putting loaves of bread into special cardboard boxes. Oh that, says my driver. When people move away from Detroit a lot of them still want our bread so we mail it to them. I can't believe it. I rush back to my office and rough out two thirty-second spots, which I leave on our art director's board.

❖

The sky over the cedars had turned to deep purple and the first Hex of the evening makes its appearance, not in the sky overhead, but on the surface of the creek. It rides the current silently and alone, the huge wings prostrate in the surface film, its body twitching, struggling as do all living things in the fight against the inevitable. It floats into the deep corner of the bend and hangs for a moment on the cedar post that had been driven into the creek by the German seaman who had jumped ship on the East Coast around the turn of the century. The German found his way to the deep pine woods of Michigan and lived his life on the edge of this swamp. There are signs of his handiwork along the creek—the pilings for what must have been a footbridge, the remnant of a small diversion dam that would have kept the water there from freezing in the winter. He knew his wood; all the pilings are cedar and will still be there at the turn of the next century.

The current sucked the big fly away from the piling and it began to float over the deepest part of the pool and I knew that eyes other than mine were watching it. But the appearance of just one fly wasn't quite enough to trigger an

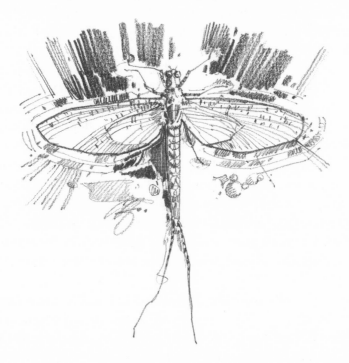

attack, and the spent Hex floated out of sight down the chute below the bend. I changed from a dun to a spinner, a pattern with double badger wings that on the water wiggle better than a hooker's ass. Even in the gloom I had no trouble making the change thanks to 0X and a #2 hook. Another fly came down and then another. Around the bend upstream I heard a splash. There were spinners falling up there but I wasn't about to move. I had business with a resident of this pool. We had parried the evening before and I suspected that if enough of these pork chops floated by his doorstep there was a good chance for a rematch. In the darkness I had not seen the trout, but if it was a brown it was a good one. If it was a brook trout, it was the grand-pappy of all brook trout. I had heard stories—on the sly of course—about the brook trout that had come out of this creek. One of the village elders, who grew up near the creek and knew the old German sailor, once confided that he had *speared* brook trout in the creek that were over *twenty inches*. Speared them for God's sake!

So I waited. Spinners began to float by in greater numbers and the kids began to slurp. I thought about my friends in the city and my children and how much I missed them all. I wanted my son to see this creek and what happens here when the Hex comes off. I recalled with pleasure the not-too-distant time I was able to put him and his two sisters—the freckled princesses—in a TV spot, the fun they had "acting" and goofing around on location. They were three of fifty extras but thought they were the stars, and that's all that counted. I also recalled a certain dog, key to a certain scene, that decided to take care of business not just during one take, but during a succession of takes. Then a car alarm went off somewhere close and the dog said *adios*. The thirty-second epic-in-the-making came to a halt while trainer, cast, and crew sprinted down a Detroit alley after a one-hundred-pound white wolfhound that appeared to have the speed of an F-15. Then the cops started badgering me about how they couldn't keep the street blocked off any longer. Then the head of the merchant's association began to scream about all the business they were losing and loudly mentioned the word "litigation." Not for the first time did I begin to have thoughts of trout streams on a permanent basis.

The big guy fed and I swear the hair stood up on the back of my head. Imagine standing next to a small creek in a swamp on a dark, quiet night. Imagine that someone you don't see throws a brick in the water near the opposite bank. Imagine the sound that brick would make—on this quiet, dark night—when it hits the water. Imagine that, and you have the sound of an outsized brown trout (God, *maybe* a brookie!) taking a Hex. Except for one thing: you can't duplicate the *savagery* of the sound. When a big trout takes a Hex the sound has overtones of barbarism that makes you think about great white sharks or man-eating tigers.

A coyote ripped a good wail close-by and I thought I was coming straight out of my waders. But I was standing and stripping line, the big pattern whizzing by my ear as I lengthened line and dropped the fly near the opposite bank. The attack was almost instantaneous and I reefed back to bury the hook. There was a tremendous gusher of water as the trout slued around to get under the bank. Just as fast it turned again and bolted upstream in six inches of water, leaving a wake that reached both banks. The reel howled, and behind me in the bushes I heard noises moving away. The trout was around the bend above and I was in the creek, running after it. At the bend the trout was still on, but I spooked it up to the next bend. This time I stood my ground and, remembering the heavy tippet, leaned on the fish. It slowed but I couldn't turn it. This bend was almost a double-back and the fly line was across the grass as the trout again tore upstream. I came around the bend and discovered the big slob heading right for the pilings of the old diversion dam, and then it was in there and that was all she wrote.

I think a fisherman is entitled to all sorts of childish behavior when he loses a large fish. Personally, I don't give a rat's ass about streamside decorum as long as I'm not bothering anyone. I think if you want to yell and swear and kick things and chuck your fly rod up the bank (or into the river) that's your business. I think those posturing bullshit artists who stand around in fly shops and say things like, "I raised my rod in salute to the big fellow and knew I'd never forget him," have either caught more big trout than all of us put together or haven't caught any.

I went down and popped a beer, and when the toes on my right foot quit hurting I went looking for my fly rod. I found it in a small stand of sumac and reeled the line in and put the light on the tippet. It was frayed about six inches from where the fly would have been. OX. I drove the truck to Jack's Place where the lovely Kim got me straightened away with a Budweiser and a double shot of bourbon. I consoled myself by reminding myself that I could go back every night all summer and try again for that trout.

As it turned out I went back plenty of times, but never hooked it again or even saw the fish feed. I have visions of a thirty-inch brown trout (sometimes it's a twenty-five-inch brookie) dying of old age, turning belly-up in that little creek out in that swamp, washing downstream with the current, lodging in some logjam or settling into the silt, the big spots fading forever. All I wanted was to see it.

Dodge City. That's how advertising people in Detroit sometimes refer to their turf, where mega-million-dollar car accounts dominate; competition is fierce and the stakes are high. I never worked directly on a car account, but I've gotten out of Dodge.

I grew up in what was then a relatively small town in northern Ohio. There were woods and fields across the road, farms five minutes to the south, and Lake Erie five minutes to the north. Growing up, I hunted and fished as much as I wanted to. I am sometimes overwhelmed that I can do it again if only in the evening. In the summer I hang out in fly shops and hustle guiding jobs. In the winter I chase words. There is still the business of keeping something in the larder and storing enough acorns to get through the winter, which in northern Michigan is long and cold.

During moments of reflection, I realize that I always knew it would come to this. You have an intuitive sense of priorities or you deliberately set them. Some people get hooked on money and power; I got hooked on woods and lakes and trout streams. And words. So no midlife crisis here, sorry to report, or any quarrel with the ad biz. I had some great times and worked with some gifted people, many of whom became good friends. But woods and water and trout kept getting in the way and increasingly I yearned for a simpler way of life. There were times on Sunday evenings or early Monday mornings as I drove south on the interstate back to the city that my depression was as big and gloomy as an empty boxcar. And I didn't need a shrink to tell me why. So here I am, but not without some pain and sacrifice, and I do not stand alone in that regard.

Reality now? Well, since you asked...

It's driving to work (a fly shop where I will meet a client) and seeing fourteen turkeys, seven deer, one porcupine, one coyote, a sharp-shinned hawk, and *not one* car in the course of twenty minutes, the record so far.

It's going to the bank where the two tellers know me and not having to produce twenty-eight pieces of identification to accomplish a simple transaction.

It's having your life depend to a large extent on the whims of mayflies, caddis flies, and stone flies. I explain to a friend that I can't come downstate to her birthday party because the brown drakes are about to come off and I'm booked. A city girl, this takes some real explaining, and she is incredulous. "Bugs! Bugs! You mean your income depends on little bugs that live in the water!"

It's Huey, my mailman, routinely delivering letters so vaguely addressed that they might read *Jim Enger, Somewhere In Northern Michigan*. Then we talk for ten minutes about my new bird-dog puppy and his new black Lab.

It's the luxury of having time to explore some wild places and finding four remote beaver ponds, three of which have brookies.

Even phone calls tend to be of a different nature. Eddie Golnick calls from his trailer on the banks of the South Branch. Eddie once knew every beaver pond in three counties but doesn't get around so well anymore. "Not floating today?" he asks.

"Not today, Ed."

"It's probably just as well. The river may be too low."

"Why do you say that?"

"Well, two trout just knocked on the door and asked for a glass of water."

2

THE GUIDE AS...

Many years ago my parents bought a place on the main branch of the Au Sable River in northern Michigan. My late father was a passionate fly fisherman and had a special fondness for this stretch of the river known far and wide as the "Holy Water."

The "cabin"—as we call it—came with furniture, seven hundred feet of frontage, and an endless number of new friends. But as a founding member of one of the country's largest fly fishing clubs, my father had a lot of friends. And all were welcome except those who showed up unannounced at the dinner hour.

The place also came with a canoe, although the river was easy to wade. Word got around and it wasn't long before I was unofficially in the guiding business on weekends, not for hire but for fun. Friends would show up and we would throw the canoe in the river and go fishing.

But if you float the Au Sable, you're really only faking it if you don't have a traditional Au Sable riverboat. These boats evolved during the logging boom of the late 1800s and were used to carry supplies up and down the river. It wasn't long before early trout and grayling fishermen were using them too.

Most of the boats are about twenty-four feet long and a yard wide. They have a flat bottom and a slight up-sweep at bow and stern. They are eminently graceful. There is a seat for the guide right at the stern and another for the angler near the front. The angler's seat is mounted above a livewell between two small storage compartments. Some long-ago genius figured out that if you made this structure an integral part of the boat, you could drill holes in the bottom of the center compartment. That compartment would then fill with water as deep as the boat rode in the river, about three inches. On most boats there is a hole on the front side of the compartment just below the angler's chair. If the sport wants to keep a trout, he simply slips it through the hole into the livewell. At the end of the float the seat is removed, followed by the trout, as fresh as you will ever get them. Now, with the popularity of catch-and-release, you're more likely to find cans of beer in the livewell.

I knew I had to have one of these boats, but they are not easy to obtain. They aren't built commercially, and used ones are hard to come by. There are a few guys near the town of Grayling who make one or two a year, and they get good money for their work, as they should.

I found mine lying in the woods near our place. It belonged to a kid who lived just upstream, and who once intended to guide. When he discovered cars and girls the riverboat was left to rot. Three of us went in together and made him an offer, and one spring weekend we found ourselves with an Au Sable riverboat built in 1941 by Herb Stephan, a guide and boatbuilder and descendant of a family that originally settled the area. With it came a trailer built on the rear chassis of a 1938 Ford, complete with spoked wheels and original Ford V-8 hubcaps.

I spent the summer stripping and refurbishing the boat with the help of my brother-in-law, Ron "Olive Matuka" Randlett, a one-third owner. Our other partner, Pete, found more excuses not to come north during weekends that summer than I knew existed. He kept from feeling guilty by handling the boat registration and trailer license. He also bought and contributed an expensive, traditional, long-handled boat net made from exotic wood. And he called me every Monday morning at work in the city and asked how our boat was coming.

A few years later I found myself in the north woods for keeps, hustling guiding business, Au Sable riverboat waiting and ready. Have boat, will float.

Years of guiding friends and occasional business associates was no preparation for being a hired gun. I had no illusions it wouldn't be work; I worked at it even when I had friends in the boat and we were fishing for fun. The good guides worked their butts off for their clients. I knew that. But there were a few things I didn't know, a few nasty little secrets the guides sometimes talk about among themselves when the moon is full and the tip money is being converted to alcohol in the local ale house. No one told me, for example, that it would be helpful to have a doctorate in psychology.

Most of the people I guided were good folks. Skill levels ran from beginner (as in: "Should the reel be up or down?") to anglers very competent in every regard (rare). But in the course of a season you find yourself in some astonishing situations. All that follows is the gospel truth, I swear to you on my one and only Wheatley.

The Guide as International Diplomat
Scene: South Branch, near Chase Bridge

The clients are Japanese, a father and son. The son, in his mid-40s, is a supervisor at a Japanese-owned American auto plant. The father is elderly and is making his first trip to America so that he can visit his son. The father speaks not one word of English. Every fly fishing gadget known to man hangs from their vests; camera bags are everywhere. The guide puts Pops in the middle of the boat, the son up front. There is no hatch so the guide rigs one rod with a streamer, the other with a parachute Adams, a good searching pattern. The son starts with the streamer and ten minutes down the river hooks a five-inch brook trout. There is pandemonium in the boat while cameras come out and the fish is photographed at least ten times to a chorus of "Ohs!" and "Ahs!"

GUIDE: Don't use up all your film on little brook trout.

Ten minutes later the same thing happens all over again.

GUIDE: Now remember, don't use up all your film on little brook trout.

Much bowing and nodding of heads.

A short time later the son sticks a brown about fourteen inches. The trout comes to the boat, there is a short, animated discussion in Japanese and *one* photo is taken before the trout goes back.

Another small brook trout and chaos again. At least a dozen photos from two cameras. The guide wonders.

Another brown trout. No photo this time.

The guide drops the anchor chain and re-rigs both rods with 5X tippets, a #16 parachute Coachman on one, a #16 Royal Trude on the other. The guide paddles past a dozen good brown trout pools to a long, shallow riffle loaded with brookies, mostly small. More than a dozen undersize brook trout come to the boat. The clients are hysterical, the cameras smoke.

For hours the guide moves the boat through good brown trout water and stops any place he thinks has brook trout. He says later it was a difficult, but stimulating effort to think in reverse.

At Dogtown a twelve-inch brookie is landed and all hell breaks loose. Two entire rolls of film are shot and Pops falls out of the boat trying to get a photo of the trout in the water.

At the end of the day the guide gets what turns out to be his biggest tip of the season.

The Guide as Child Psychologist
Scene: North Branch, near the Sheep Ranch

The clients are a father and son who have booked a clinic. Dad wants a tune-up and the son, age fourteen, is to be introduced to fly fishing. The goal is to have the boy casting reasonably well and beginning to read water by the end of the day. The guide has done this many, many times.

The guide is somewhat suspicious when he has to tell the boy that the jam box and tapes can't come along. There is a minor temper tantrum, but the boom box remains at the lodge.

At the river sonnyboy complains that his waders don't fit right. The guide rigs up a rod for junior, explaining how everything goes together, while junior stares off into the woods.

Most of the morning is spent with the boy, who spends most of his time asking if it's lunchtime yet. He does the opposite of everything the guide tells him. The guide is considering a discussion with Dad about attitude but decides to hold off, hoping junior will actually catch a trout, which often does the trick.

At lunchtime Dad stands on shore and watches sonnyboy throw the fly. Over sandwiches, Dad has a few not-so-subtle questions about the guide's teaching ability.

Back at it again and Dad, all tuned up, works his way downstream. The guide puts junior in an easy pool and starts at the beginning again. Junior looks smug as he slaps the water fore and aft and yet another fly snaps off. He grins. Then the guide grabs him by the back of the neck, hard. Junior's eyeballs pop.
GUIDE: Look, you little bastard, I'm sick of your bullshit. I'm going to shove your greasy little head in the river and

let you count nymphs for a couple of minutes if you don't get your act together.

Moments later junior is throwing loops that would make Lefty Kreh proud. At the end of the day, there is another review of junior's progress.

DAD: Now that's better.

GUIDE: Sometimes it just all comes together at once.

The Guide as Drug Enforcement Officer
Scene: Main branch, near Guide's Rest

The "client" is an old friend of the guide. The guide has offered to float him for free since the guide has no booking that day. But the old friend insists on paying *something,* maybe gas money for the pickup, because he knows that the guide must make a living and the season is short. Some of the guide's acquaintances think that the guide is thrilled to death to float them down the river for free every time they show up on his doorstep. The guide has been working on this, tactfully in most cases, not so tactfully in others.

But today the guide himself wants to fish, a true busman's holiday, and is happy to have company. Sulphur Duns have been coming good for three days and the fishing has been wonderful. The guide and his friend put in at Louie's Landing and plan to float to Wakeley Bridge. The old riverboat is loaded with beer, bourbon, hibachi, steaks, potatoes, onions, etc. Two bottles of burgundy clink together in the livewell—referred to today as the automatic, self-cooling wine cellar. If five dams weren't in the way, the guide and his friend could float clear to the mouth of the Au Sable and across Lake Huron to Canada with the provisions that are on board.

The Sulphurs turn out to be spotty, but there are enough trout looking up and the fishing is terrific. The guide and his friend decide to stop at Guide's Rest to indulge in serious food and drink. Guide's Rest is a little meadow on the north bank of the river that has been used as a lunch stop by the guides for decades. It is also a memorial to Jim Wakeley, one of the famous Michigan riverguides, who died in his boat.

As the guide begins to pole the boat over to the bank, there is a commotion upstream. There is hooting and hollering, jam boxes blaring and the all-too-familiar sound of canoe paddles banging on aluminum. It is supposed to be too early in the year for a serious canoe hatch, but here they come, a whole gaggle of them. Two of them collide and tip over and the contents of both canoes goes into the river, an ordinary event. The guide drops the anchor chain and grabs the long-handle, boat net and prepares to snare as much floating trash as he can.

Two or three beer cans are quickly snagged, along with the Styrofoam top to a cooler. And then, lo and behold, and floating high and dry, comes a zip-lock bag full of pot. The stash is easily snared by the guide. A moment later the canoes begin to pass the anchored riverboat. In the last canoe are two wet, ugly, pimply-faced, drunk morons—your average commercial canoeists. The only thing missing is a fat woman.

MORON IN STERN: You got my stash, asshole?

The guide, who was leaning toward compassion, thus has his mind made up for him. The guide holds the bag aloft and smiles.

MORON IN BOW: C'mon man, throw us the bag!

The guide puts the pot in his shirt pocket. It is a big bag and barely fits.

MORON IN BOW: Hey shithead, you can't keep that!

The guide smiles again. His friend is laughing.

MORON IN BOW: Hey man, we'll trade you some beers for it!

The guide smiles, holds his own Budweiser aloft. The current carries the canoe, with its hideous crew, downstream and out of sight. But the guide and his friend can hear them for several minutes, screaming obscenities. Finally they are also out of earshot.

The guide smiles again.

The Guide as Celebrity Tour Guide
Scene: Main branch, near Camp Ginger Quill

The client this day is an enthusiastic novice who is fishing the Au Sable for the first time. He has been to the Orvis fly fishing school and has been buying and reading every book about fly fishing he can get his hands on. His list of heroes is already long: Brooks, Bates, Schwiebert, Traver, Kreh, Haig-Brown, McClane, Lee, Waterman, Lyons. The guide hears about all of them. But above all, he hears about Carl and Doug. For today the client is going to float the *very water* which helped give birth to *Selective Trout*. Swisher and Richards are kings for this day. They are what brought the novice a long distance to the river. The guide silently thanks Doug and Carl.

The plan is to float from Stephan Bridge to Wakeley Bridge. When the guide picks the client up at the lodge, the client opens *Selective Trout* and points to photos of insects on pages that have been marked with paper clips. The client wants to know if he has timed his arrival to coincide with the hatches he has marked. The guide stares seriously at the photos and nods his head.

CLIENT: Oh, wow!

The client is full of questions and full of Doug and Carl. His fly boxes are jammed with no-hackle flies. *Selective Trout* gets a thorough analysis down the river. This is perhaps the guide's favorite sort of client—for the enthusiasm, for the chance to share a little of what he knows, for the knowledge that each trout brought to the boat will be a major victory. So the guide cheerfully puts up with the running discourse on Doug and Carl and *Selective Trout*. The client asks the guide if he has met Doug and/or Carl?

GUIDE: Swisher once, Richards a few times.

CLIENT: Oh, wow!

Then, as if right on cue, the guide and client come round a bend and not thirty yards downstream is Carl himself, fishing away. The guide isn't surprised because Carl belongs to a club right around the next bend. With lowered voice the guide tells the client just who that is standing in the river down there.

CLIENT: No!

GUIDE: Yep.

CLIENT: Carl Richards!?

GUIDE: Yep.

The riverboat draws abreast of Richards.

GUIDE: Hi Carl, howya doing?

CARL: Not bad. How about yourself?

GUIDE: We're getting a few.

CARL: Same here.

The guide and the client float on by. The client is thunderstruck and his fly line trails in the water, his jaw somewhere around the middle of his chest.

CLIENT: I don't believe it. That was Carl Richards! Unbelievable!

The client sits in the front of the boat shaking his head. The guide sits in the back of the boat wondering what it is about fly fishing that produces groupies possibly more impassioned than the nut cases who follow rock bands. Carl didn't know it, but Bon Jovi never had a fan as devoted as the fly fisherman sitting in the bow of the riverboat.

The gods were certainly smiling that day upon the eager client. Around the very next bend was the other half of the team, throwing those candycane loops for which he is famous. The guide was surprised to see Doug, who—as legend had it—was supposed to have forsaken Michigan for the West. Rumors put Doug somewhere in Montana doing fly fishing schools and producing videos.

GUIDE: Psssssssst!

Client turns in seat, guide points downstream.

CLIENT: What?

GUIDE: There's Doug.

Client spins around, smacks fly rod on bow. The riverboat draws abreast of Swisher.

DOUG: Hi fellahs. Any luck?

GUIDE: We're getting a few.

DOUG: Great! Nice day isn't it.

Riverboat floats on downstream.

CLIENT: I can't believe it! My God! This is unreal! Wait 'till I tell the guys back home! Unbelievable! Who could have guessed! I should have brought my book. I could have had both of them sign it!

The guide wonders about the propriety of stopping a riverboat midstream to ask wading authors for autographs.

At the end of the day the guide gets what turns out to be his second-biggest tip of the season.

The Guide as Marriage Counselor

Scene: Main branch, near Pine Road access

The clients are a husband and wife. She is a bank executive; he has been unemployed for seven months, having lost his job when his firm relocated. She is footing the bill for the float trip. The guide detects an undercurrent of tension when he picks them up at the fly shop. She will not fish but will sit in the center seat and take photos.

In terms of fishing, the trip begins well. The angling client takes a number of fair browns and brookies on dry flies. The nonangling client is sullen and snipes at her husband.

At noon the guide poles the boat to the bank, where he will serve lunch on a friendly dock. The guide knows that the nonangling client has brought a bottle of wine and the guide is leery. The guide breaks out the lunch, she uncorks the wine. In minutes the wine takes effect.

SHE (To guide): I'm not sure why I agreed to this. We don't have money to throw around these days.

The guide mumbles something.

SHE: He hasn't worked a damn day in seven months.

HE: C'mon, I don't think our guide really wants to hear about this.

SHE: You couldn't even pay for your fishing license!

HE: For crissake, let's not start.

SHE (To guide): You think he could find something to do besides sit home all day long.

Guide mumbles something, dishes up potato salad.

SHE: We'll just have our little float trip today, and then Monday morning when we get home you're going to get on the damn telephone and start calling people.

HE: I'm not going to start begging for a job!

SHE: It's called networking, not begging!

HE: I've already called everyone that got a resume!

SHE: You're going to call them all again!

HE: Like hell!

SHE: You're a damn freeloader!

HE: I've worked all my life!

SHE: Bullshit!

The dialog continues in this vein for several minutes, volume increases.

GUIDE (Jumps up, slams lid on cooler): That's it folks! You keep your money! Everybody back in the boat!

Complete silence. The guide paddles furiously to the Pine Road access, puts fun couple out with directions to pay phone.

HE (To guide): I don't blame you.

The guide continues down the river, now able to fish, and wishes he had some beer. The guide resolved years ago, in a different life, never again to be a participant in conversations like the one he just heard. On the river, he is not even going to be a listener. Near Black Bend he runs into a wading friend who wonders why the guide is alone in his riverboat. The friend laughs like hell when the guide explains. The guide invites the friend to float. The friend has a six-pack stashed in a logjam, which now goes into the cooler in the boat. The guide and his friend float down the river drinking beer, eating potato salad and roast beef sandwiches. And catching trout. Victory is snatched from the jaws of defeat.

The Guide as a Pin Cushion
Scene: South Branch, near the Highbanks

Today's client is an affable middle-aged man who wants to fish dry flies only. The client strings up three cane rods that have impeccable pedigrees: a Leonard, a Payne, and a Paul H. Young. At the landing the client begins telling jokes which—as it turns out—he will do all day. He is a good storyteller, the jokes are fresh and the guide is greatly entertained.

Fancy rods or not, the client's casting is a bit rusty and the guide finds himself ducking as flies whiz by his ears. The guide determines that a warning is necessary.

GUIDE: Now don't forget, I'm sitting twenty feet behind you. Watch your backcast.

CLIENT: Don't worry, I won't hook you.

Every guide on the Au Sable and Manistee River systems has heard the phrase, "don't worry, I won't hook you," a thousand times. In fly shops on these rivers you can tell who the guides are by examining the backs of shirts. The guides will be the guys with a lot of little holes and rips and tears in their shirts where flies have been cut out. It goes with the turf.

Finally it happens. There is a good midstream riser and the backcast is low and deadly. The guide feels the hook bite into his shoulder.

GUIDE: Hold it!

CLIENT: Oh Jesus!

The guide drops the anchor chain and lays the pushpole down and attempts to find the fly, but cannot reach it.

GUIDE: I'm going to come up front. You'll have to get this out. I'll tell you what to do.

CLIENT: Believe it or not, I'm a doctor.

GUIDE: Glory be. It's through my shirt and into the skin.

It turns out that Doc had forgotten to pinch the barb down on this particular fly and, as usual, there is knifework on the guide's shirt and just a little bit on his skin.

After some fuss, the fly comes out and the float trip continues. When the client gets over his embarrassment the jokes start again and the float turns out to be a good one. The client manages not to hook the guide a second time.

Two weeks after the trip the guide opens his mail and finds a bill. "For professional services, hook removal...$450.00. Thank You."

The guide pays it with Monopoly money.

3

❖

FLY FISHING'S
SEVEN BIGGEST MYTHS

Rumors abound that fly fishing is "coming of age." From campfires along the Umpqua to the old private clubs on the Beaverkill, one hears solemn conversations proclaiming that our sport has reached its zenith. This coming-of-age thing is not new. It used to happen maybe once in a generation, and most often was tied to new technology. *Humph! Fly rods made out of little strips of bamboo! Never work!* Then fly fishing began reaching its zenith more often—maybe once or twice a decade. *What do you mean you don't have to dry the fly line! Who says you don't have to soak your leaders!* Still more zeniths more often. *Fiberglass, eh? Good lord, now everyone will be able to do it! Knotless leaders? Seems like cheating!* Finally, it seemed as though we were reaching new zeniths about every six months. *Graphite, eh? Looks a little on the flimsy side. Don't think I'll throw away my glass rods. It's called what—Flashabou? Hey, cool! It's called a what—a Zonker? Far out!*

So what's next? Who knows. But a guy I know is already experimenting with a hand-held GPS unit to mark new beaver ponds. GPS, or Global Positioning System, is a navigational aid that receives signals from an orbiting chain of Department of Defense satellites and will pinpoint your location within yards anywhere on the planet. There are miniature versions you can carry with you. Our guys used them in the Persian Gulf War to chase the nasty Iraqis.

Personally, I'm sticking to discreet little blaze marks on trees, and to my topo maps, despite the risk. And despite the mushroom-picker/tree-hugger type who once accused me of "maiming" our wonderful green "friends." And in spite of the fact that I have nightmares about my maps falling into the wrong hands.

While technology as it's connected to our game zips along like a Stealth fighter, our rituals, customs, and traditions move like a Sopwith Camel, which is just fine with me. But this has created a lot of confusion, especially among newcomers to the sport. Even some older hands are in a state these days. I want to help dispel some of the bewilderment that's out there. You ask: what makes you think you're qualified to offer advice? To which I reply: I've spent a good part of the last two decades staying up late, beverage at hand, contemplating the issues, large and small, that confront our treasured avocation. So I must say that I feel particularly qualified to throw in my two cents. On one grave issue you'll see that even *I* wasn't sure; so in the interest of solid investigative reporting, as well as science, of course, I consulted an expert.

Let me attempt to dispel some of the myths that currently confront our sacred pastime:

Myth #1—That Trout Taste Worse Than Fruitcake
This is one of the biggest issues that faces fly fishing today. How this myth got started no one seems to know. A major university recently conducted a research program to study the behavioral patterns of trout fishermen. Three groups of trout fishermen were convened in separate focus groups. The first group interviewed had been fly fising for ten to twenty years. The second group had been fly fishing for five to ten years. The third group had been fly fishing one to five years.

When asked the question, "Have you ever eaten a trout?" the first group (ten to twenty years' fly fishing) were observed to smile; a discussion followed, mostly centering around recipes and various wines. Chardonnay was mentioned by four of the fifteen subjects, Chablis by seven

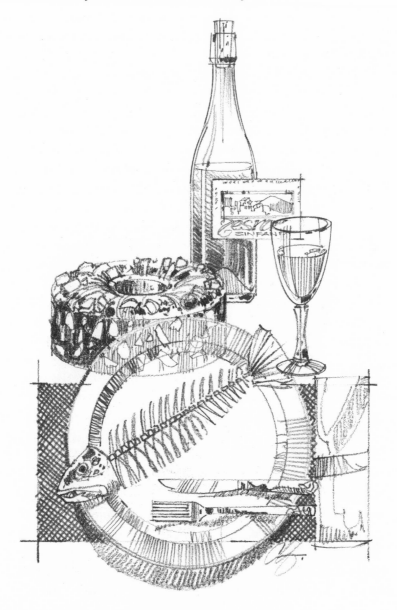

(including one French Grand Cru—Les Clos—by label), Zinfandel by two, Beaujolais by one, and Vouvray by one.

When asked, "What do trout taste like?" the subjects used a variety of phrases and descriptive words. "Awe-inspiring," "wondrous," "savor," and "piquancy" were among the words used.

When asked the question, "Have you ever eaten a trout?" the second group (fly fishing five to ten years) was observed to be uncomfortable. Several participants fidgeted in their chairs. Three excused themselves to go to the men's room. Four of the fifteen said they had eaten trout in restaurants. (Which, for the purposes of the research, was invalid.)

Finally one subject, looking flushed, said he had eaten a wild trout. Other group members were then observed to edge away from him and seemed even more uncomfortable.

When the single respondent was asked, "What do trout taste like?" he said he couldn't remember.

The third group (fly fishing one to five years) was interviewed in the same manner as the other two.

In response to the first question, "Have you ever eaten a trout?" three of the subjects fainted, four began to hyperventilate (causing no small amount of alarm among the staff—911 was called) and the remainder were visibly pale, shaken, and were observed to take on a hostile demeanor.

No respondent admitted to having eaten a trout, so the second question was rephrased: "What do you *think* a trout might taste like?" (At this point the session was interrupted by the EMS crews. The session eventually resumed.) "Worse than fruitcake!" "Like pig slop!" "They're poisonous!" "Like cat do-do!" These were some of the phrases used by those remaining in the third group regarding what they *thought* trout must taste like.

Obviously, a trend had been identified. It appeared that trout were losing their taste. The reason why, of course, was the big question. The possibilities are ominous. It occurred to me that I should eat a trout in the interest of research, but the season being closed just then, it wasn't in the cards. Then I had an inspiration. I called a Native-American friend who eats trout from time to time, and who, most likely, had a few in the freezer.

"Billy," I asked, "have you got any trout?"

"You want some?"

"Just tell me, when was the last time you had trout?"

"A couple of days ago. Why?"

"How were they?"

"What do you mean how were they? They were good."

"Tell me, do trout taste as good today as they did, say, ten years ago?"

There was a long pause. "Are you all right man?"

"Just answer the question."

"Are you crazy? Why wouldn't they? Why do you want to know this?"

So I told him about the university study.

"I can't speak to it. Maybe the trout down your way have something wrong with them. The trout up this way are still tastin' pretty good. Want me to overnight you some?"

"That's okay. I was just checking."

Thankfully the season finally opened. I tippy-toed into my favorite beaver pond and corralled a couple of brookies. (A small Royal Trude did the trick.) All the way home—as I tried in vain to keep my salivating glands in neutral—I wondered if they would taste okay. It was a moment fraught with anxiety as I began to prepare them using a timeworn, trusty recipe:

1. Dress two or more brook trout (removing the heads is your option—the little fleck of meat in the cheek is delicious).
2. Heat a thin film of peanut oil in a large frying pan.
3. Dip the trout in milk and then roll in flour.

4. Place a few thin slices of apple in the cavity and seal with a toothpick.

5. Brown the trout on both sides on moderate high heat until skin is crispy.

6. Put the trout on dishes, or serving platter, and keep warm.

7. Add a quarter stick of butter to the juices in the frying pan. Mix together and cook until the butter begins turning brown. Pour over trout.

8. Garnish with a few pearl onions laid alongside, baby carrots, or your favorite greens.

I am relieved to tell you that those trout did not taste worse than fruitcake. In fact, I thought they were pretty damned good. Delicious even. But that's my opinion. I included the recipe here so that you can dispel this particularly horrific myth yourself.

Myth #2—That It's Okay to Wear Your Fishing Vest to Dinner in the Lodge Dining Room

You would think that wearing your vest all day long while fishing would be enough. But no, here and there we're starting to see vests *at table* in the dining rooms at various fishing lodges around the country. This seems to be a trend among younger fishermen, so maybe this is one of those so-called yuppie things.

I recently saw a young chap (mid-twenties I guessed) in the dining room of a noted lodge on Michigan's Au Sable River. He was wearing a teal-colored vest. (Perhaps that's a clue.) He was well along with his entrée, a generous portion of prime rib. I caught myself wondering if he might dribble on his fleece patch, which abounded with flies. (I could see the headlines in the hook-and-bullet magazines: Au Jus Better than Dr. Juice!) At any rate, what's perplexing about this is that normally you wear your vest over your wader straps. Which means that at the end of the fishing you must remove the vest in order to get out of your waders. In order to wear your vest to dinner you would, obviously, have to put it back on. So, it's not as though any of these transgressors could have simply forgotten to shed their vests.

What's the story here? I didn't know, so I put the issue to Judith Martin, aka Miss Manners, whose column on etiquette appears in newspapers all over the country. From her tony perch on New York's Park Avenue came this reply: "Even the *fish* [emphasis hers!] is expected to change for dinner, putting on something more appropriate, such as hollandaise."

So there you are. No more fishing vests at the lodge dinner table, teal or otherwise.

Myth #3—That You Must Speak Latin in Order to Fly Fish

Back in the dark ages of fly fishing (and fly tying), when our predecessors were dumb and unenlightened, bugs were often referred to as "little brown ones" or "that tiny black one" or "the bitty yellow thing."

But how much fun can you have saying "little gray bugger" when, instead, you can say *"Paraleptophlebia adoptiva?"* Apparently many, if not most fly fishermen, liked the way the latter rolled off the tongue. It wasn't long before you'd hear an exchange like this along our trout streams.

FIRST FISHERMAN (pointing to a collecting screen): There was a lot of detritus in the substrate, but I turned up some *Stenonema ithica* and a few *Ephemera varia*.

SECOND FISHERMAN: That's odd, I thought it was *Stenonema interpunctatum* that was active, but then I was sampling in a depositional zone. I did pick up a few *Siphlonurus quebecensis* though.

Well, pretty soon everybody was talking like that. And, it was apparent that there were a lot of wonderful things associated with the New Way.

For example, if you were filling out a job application you could reply "yes" to the question, "Do you speak a second language?" And guys would write in something like *"Cheumatopsyche gracilus!"* just to prove it.

Bugbook publishing took off like a rocket. Thousands of books appeared overnight. These had page after page of little pictures of bugs which, if you studied them for weeks and months, you could actually see the difference between some of them.

Dime stores suddenly did a land-office business in magnifying glasses.

Aspirin sales skyrocketed.

And of course sales of collecting screens and insect nets soared.

Then, too, it tended to keep out the worm fishermen. Those who might have converted were too intimidated and decided to stick with their own game where "gimme a dozen crawlers" pretty much covered the waterfront. (Thankfully, I gave up garden hackle and slipped in under the wire just before the advent of the New Way. I shudder to think that the double-compartment Wheatley reposing on my desk with all its fuzzy little residents might, instead, be a cottage cheese container in a back corner of the refrigerator.)

Finally, my Catholic fly fishing friends discovered that if you were taking a meal in the dining room of a lodge that catered to fly fishermen, you could close your eyes and be right back in church during the good old days. It sounded just the same.

Eventually I, too, thought it would be more fun to talk Latin. I spent a fortune on books and sat up nights memorizing the names of hundreds of bugs. And like any new convert, I was eager to impress everybody that I met.

Take the time I was fishing downstream from the Pine Road access on the main branch of the Au Sable River. It was a fine summer evening and I could see a guy working his way upstream. He was taking trout after trout on a big glass rod. He was wearing an old flannel shirt and his waders were tied around his belly. I sensed that he was a "local" and moved off to one side to let him pass. He turned out to be a friendly sort, and as he drew near he nodded, said hello, and asked how I was doing.

I leapt at the chance. "I caught a couple on this *Pseudocloeon anoka* imitation a little earlier," I said smugly, holding up the fly.

He caught his leader and examined a very bedraggled fly. "I've been knocking the piss out of them with this little green shitter." He lit a Camel and continued upstream.

Myth #4—That It's Okay to Pee in the Stream

Never. A Michigan fisherman was cited for "discharging untreated sewage into a river," having been caught with his waders around his knees by a conservation officer.

Myth #5—That Fly Fishing is Difficult

One August day a few years ago I came around a bend on the North Branch of the Au Sable. It was a glorious summer day and I was floating from pool to pool in my graceful little thirteen-foot Stowe. There was a small girl in the river fishing. She was in full costume, right up to flies on the fleece patch, and graphite rod. While I watched she threw a nice loop downstream, checked her cast, and her dry fly landed gently on the water. The fly floated a yard or so and was taken by a trout. She deftly set the hook, wound in her loose line, and played the trout off the reel. She kept her tip up, coolly battled the trout, backed up into the shallows, got the fish in, and then used her forceps to remove the hook. She gently held the fish facing upstream until it darted away. I let the canoe drift abreast of her.

"Nice job," I said. "How long have you been fly fishing?"

"I just started this summer," she replied.

"That's a pretty nice outfit you've got there."

"My dad gave it to me when I graduated from Lower School in June."

Myth #6—That It's Okay To Smoke On Trout Streams

It is impossible these days to ignore this ugly and depressing subject. But I would feel remiss if I let this slide. Let me give you some background:

For many years I smoked a pipe. In fact, I "took up" pipe smoking in high school when I worked in a drugstore in my then-small town in northern Ohio. One of my duties was the tobacco counter and one of the tobacco salesmen slipped me freebies—pipes and a variety of the stuff you put in them. I was easily corrupted and displayed that salesman's products in the most prominent places. At that time I was mostly in pursuit of perch and white bass on Lake Erie, and I was probably the only sixteen-year-old pipe-smoking fisherman on the lake, at least in my neck of the woods. I thought I was pretty cool, tooling around the lake or in my '56 Olds, clouds of Cherry Blend spewing from my Doctor Grabow.

One autumn day, years later, on a little trout stream in northern Michigan, I took a momentary break from the fishing. This was a peach of a little stream and no big secret really. But it was some trouble to get to the better stretches and I rarely saw another fisherman. Believe it or not, a guy in a bar in Indian River, Michigan, told me about it. It was in this very same bar a few years later, after a day of steelheading, that I somehow found myself in the midst of one of those classic brawls you see in the old Western movies. Only these were a bunch of drunken deer hunters. About all I remember is that I broke a beautiful turquoise ring I had bought in Taxco, Mexico, on some guy's face. I was waiting at the door when the joint opened the next day and crawled around the floor on my hands and knees searching for the stones. The sweeper, however, had done his work well. But I'm digressing.

Intelligence gathered in saloons is usually suspect and I almost didn't check out the tip. But I did, and to my surprise, the stream turned out to be even lovelier than the generous local had described it. And it was loaded with brook trout.

Anyhow, I was taking my break in a scenic little run that was about knee deep. I had been using a wet fly and I let it trail downstream as I put my rod under my arm and packed a pipe with a fresh bowl of tobacco. I fired it up with my lighter and was just taking those first few satisfying puffs when a trout nailed the trailing fly. It seemed a decent size—not a dink, which is usually the case. In my surprise, and in my haste to get the rod in my hand, I inadvertently let go of the pipe that had been clenched in my teeth. The pipe dropped straight down the front of my waders and lodged at the crotch. Mind you, it was full of hot coals. I plunged my free hand down the front of my waders only to knock coals loose and the pipe itself down the right wader leg. There was only one thing to do. I leaned over and began to splash water down the front of my waders. Still, there was a dramatic temperature increase in the region of my crotch. Desperate measures were called for. I sank to my knees, pushed the top of the waders down as far as I could, and let the water pour in. It never occurred to me to turn around and face upstream, which would have been better.

I was instantly rewarded with a hissing sound. A moment later I stood, waders puffed up like a week-old corpse thanks to gallons of river water. I looked down and expected to see water trickling from the waders. But everything seemed all right. Later, though, I would discover that my jeans were badly singed, right in a spot that would prove difficult to explain. As I turned to waddle to shore I discovered I had company. There on the bank was an older gentleman in fishing gear who had obviously walked in on the same trail I used. He looked at me and said, "I'm not sure what's going on here, but I've been fishing for almost forty years and that's the first time I've seen anyone *trying* to get water in their waders."

There you have it. Smoking on trout streams is hazardous to your health.

Myth #7—That You Should Always Wear a Wader Belt
Not unless you smoke.

4

DINNER WITH PETE

When I first got to know the Boardman River I had another, secret, name for it. My private name for it was the "Compromise River."

I called it that because the Boardman ultimately empties into Grand Traverse Bay, an arm of Lake Michigan, right in downtown Traverse City, a sophisticated northern Michigan resort town known for—among other things—its shopping. Once upon a time, when I had to be concerned about such things, I could drop the lady in my life in town with the cash and scoot a few miles out of town for some fishing. So everybody was happy, more or less. Though sometimes I would get, "But I thought we were going to spend our vacation *together!*" Never mind that there are 168 hours in a week and I was going to hog a mere 6 of them for myself. Besides, I would tell her, when you're having lunch on the terrace at the Bean Pot, look down at the river and remember that the water you're seeing flowed right around my waders a little earlier. It's sort of like being together.

That's how I came to secretly call the Boardman the "Compromise River." You can bet that I had dozens of no-compromise rivers all over the state, but trout streams being what they are, you don't usually find them flowing through the basements of designer-label boutiques. The

Boardman is a real Christian river in that regard and I was thrilled to discover its benefits. I even thought about presenting a marketing proposal to the Chamber of Commerce—"SHE SHOPS/YOU FISH!"—but had second thoughts when I realized the idea was self-defeating in the long term. True, the local merchants might have been grateful. But I couldn't imagine a trout fisherman on every bend of the river for one thing. For another, I'd know that they were stooping to my level of sickness—paying (literally) for a few stolen moments. It wasn't a club I wanted to start.

The Boardman really does flow right through downtown Traverse City and actually gets a limited salmon and steelhead run. The salmon are captured at a permanent harvesting station and stripped of their eggs, practically in the shadow of Milliken's Department Store. At certain times of the year you'll see mom and dad and the kids with their noses pressed against the viewing windows of the egg-stripping station, Gucci shopping bags overflowing. I swear I once saw a guy cooling his credit cards in one of the raceways.

The steelhead are passed by the weir, and one of the hot spots is the park behind the main post office, although there's not much cover there and the fish are real spooky. (If you're fly fishing on the boardwalk on the post office side, you must roll cast. Otherwise your backcast will hit the building.) But I once saw a kid not more than seven or eight years old hook what appeared to be about an eight-pounder on a Snoopy rod. His buddies dropped their rods, with their lines still in the river, and ran shrieking up and down the bank following the action. The kid's line was soon tangled in the others and a rod shot off the bank as the startled fish made a lengthy run. After two or three minutes the fish threw the hook and the kid retrieved a tangled mess of monofilament and the other Snoopy rod. His buddies offered high-fives while shouting "awesome, awesome!" And to think, some of us started out on sunfish.

I've caught steelhead off the sandbar at the mouth of the river right behind the Holiday Inn, once in a suit and tie. In an earlier life I used to get to Grand Traverse City on business and once—having been through a serious nonfishing spell—I pulled into the parking lot of the Holiday Inn, popped the trunk, pulled on my waders, and grabbed my rod. Two minutes later I was waist-deep in Traverse Bay, and about five lucky minutes after that I was fast to a small steelhead that had mistaken my Mepps spinner for a cocktail-hour hors d'oeuvre. I presented the trout to the chef at the Holiday Inn, who promised me his best effort. (Yes, there were guests who seemed skittish at the appearance of a man in waders walking through the lobby and dining room with a largish, still-wet fish.) I checked in at the front desk, and not long after that I was at the bar in the cocktail lounge, contemplating a wonderful dinner and thinking kind thoughts about a firm that would send one of its employees to Traverse City, Michigan. The bartender said—as he set my martini down—"I just heard that some jerk walked through the restaurant in waders."

South of Traverse City the river flows through the lovely Boardman valley, finding its way through mixed pine and hardwoods, and then through meadow land. Here it's a trout stream and a pretty good one if you know its secrets. Over the years it had become a favorite, and my buddy Pete and I fished it often. We liked it as an occasional alternative to the Au Sable and other rivers that could get crazy with canoes on holiday weekends. We stayed at a strange place called Ranch Rudolph—in the summer a combination midwestern dude ranch, campground, sometimes fishing camp, and in the winter a roaring snowmobile enclave. The river runs through the grounds and I especially liked the isolated, narrow meadow stretch just below the ranch. Now there is a privately owned horse operation on one side of the river where over-grazing has turned that once-pretty little meadow into a hellish mess.

But there are miles of good water. From above the ranch to Brown Bridge Pond it's mostly woodsy. Just upstream from where the river enters Brown Bridge Pond (really a small lake) Pete once caught an enormous brown trout during the Hex hatch. But the river has deep holes there and you have to know what you're doing. Especially at night. Below Brown Bridge Pond and downstream from Garfield Road, there's a lot of meadow water where grasshopper patterns can be deadly during the late summer months. Bob Summers, the famous bamboo rod maker, lives and works on this stretch.

Early one Saturday, just before first light, Pete parked the car on a turnoff in the woods above the ranch. We had pulled an all-nighter, leaving Detroit at the bewitching hour. Pete drove; I kept the coffee coming.

For those of you who have done this, you'll know that there are intermittent lapses throughout the night that are potentially fatal when the driver and the navigator have them simultaneously. For those of you who haven't, you might remember all-nighters for high school or college exams. You'll recall drifting off, and then waking with a start. But safely at your desk. It's another thing to wake up on the wrong side of the road in the deadly glare of oncoming highbeams and the desperate roar of an eighteen-wheeler's horn. This in the cause of the supposedly gentle sport. (The adrenaline rush is about the same as your first Atlantic salmon on a dry fly.)

We rigged up in the dim pale of the trunklight. I was uncertain what to start with and finally settled on a slender streamer, a Black-Nosed Dace. I couldn't see what Pete was tying on, but I knew it would be something wet. We spoke in whispers, as though not wanting to wake the red squirrels, or the tiny chickadees, or the big black bear surely sleeping just behind yonder bush.

The plan was to fish downstream, leapfrogging each other, and end up at the ranch precisely at cocktail hour late that afternoon. There we would corral someone from the ranch to drive us back to the car, something they were always glad to do.

We got in near a giant old white pine that leaned precariously across the river. Many of its branches were rusty brown, a sure sign that the tree was nearing the end of its long life. These old warrior white pines still exist

here and there, memorials left over from Michigan's incredible post–Civil War logging boom. There has been a lot written about the early logging industry in Michigan, but in his wonderful little book *Waiting for the Morning Train,*

Bruce Catton, the noted Civil War historian, wrote about growing up in Michigan and visiting some of the camps as a young man. Catton puts the Michigan logging industry in perspective, writing that enough pine boards were produced in Michigan by 1897 to build ten million six-room houses. That's one hundred and sixty billion feet of lumber, according to Catton. Michigan was literally awash in big timber. The preferred tree was the white pine. There were millions of them, they grew tall and straight, and they floated high in the shallow rivers of Michigan, making them the easiest to drive to the mills. By the early 1900s what had been one of the densest stands of pine east of the Mississippi River had been mostly leveled. Michigan had been transformed from a land of deep forest to a land of scrub.

The root mass of this big pine was pulling away from the bank and its tentacles were alive with ants, spiders, and other small critters. But it was very shallow there and no trout would hold under that potential smorgasbord, at least not with daylight coming on. So I stuck with my Dace and waded downstream, working out line and getting my arm loosened up. Minnows scattered and I felt pretty good about the fly. There was a nice little morning breeze and the sun was just beginning to break through the forest. Shafts of light did pirouettes on the river's surface. I watched Pete slide quietly into a pool of diamonds just downstream.

My first trout came to the Dace from a small pool below a snarl of tag alder. It was a brown, not large—as none of the fish in this stretch would be. It was a beautifully colored trout and I held it up and whistled. Downstream Pete smiled and gave me a thumbs-up.

I was very pleased, as I always am, with my first trout of the day. Sure, there is the satisfaction of knowing that—at least momentarily—you've got the right fly. Moreover, it's also knowing that things are right with the world, at least in my little corner of it. After that first trout, especially if it has any size to it, my anxiety level drops tremendously. Suddenly I'm hearing birds, aware of water noises, smelling the smells of the forest, and actually realizing that I have a cigar in my mouth and am tasting it.

I released the fish and watched it scoot back into the pool. I climbed out and walked the bank down to Pete. I had the thermos in the back of my vest.

"That was the icebreaker," Pete said. "What was it?"

I told him. "You want some coffee?"

Pete was warming to his task. He was working a small logjam. Cast, strip, strip, strip, cast, strip, strip, strip—and so on—until something or nothing happens. We have fished together for years and he is an intense fisherman for the first couple of hours. But not competitive. (He once caught three, twenty-five-pound steelhead on the same day on a visit to a British Columbia river, which I learned about practically by accident months later.) We glory in each other's successes, large and small.

"What I'd really like is a beer," he said. "I feel like I've been up all night."

"Well, we have been except for one little indiscretion."

"That could have been a serious whoops," he said. And then, a little pointedly, "Why don't you sit the hell down or move back. You're casting a shadow on my pool here." Subtlety is another of his attributes.

I did, in fact, find a very comfortable spot on the bank where, after unslinging my vest, I poured some coffee, relit the cigar, and enjoyed the beginnings of a beautiful day. I watched Pete work the little jam. His fly landed next to a log and there was a wonderful boil and he was fast to a fish. The trout zipped out into the current, changed its mind, and charged back toward the jam. Pete led it carefully away from the logs and minutes later had it in hand, a twin of the brown I had caught earlier.

He admired it for a moment or two and slipped it back in the water. It darted back under the logjam.

I asked Pete what he was using. He held it up as he waded to the bank. He was smiling. A Royal Coachman streamer.

"Now I'll have some coffee. But I'd rather have a beer. You got any more of those cigars?"

"This is the last one."

"Right."

He reached toward my mouth and I swatted his hand away. Then he was going through my vest.

"That's what I thought!" he said, unwrapping the dark A. C. Grenadier. "Two packs! And here's the lighter."

It was warming rapidly and I took off my jacket and stuffed it in the cargo pocket in my vest, noting that a package of cigars had disappeared.

"You're welcome," I said.

"Thank you," he replied, grinning like a lotto winner.

"Need anything else while I'm at it?"

"I think I'm fine for now," he said, blowing a puff of smoke. "Unless there's a beer in there." I shook my head.

"Then maybe you'd walk back to the car for the cooler?"

I flicked my still-lit cigar butt at his waders. He was laughing as he jumped out of the way. So was I. It was going to be a great day.

We fished downstream, doing exactly what we had planned, with a lot of jazz going back and forth about who was getting the better water. There were intermittent requests for cold beer. We each picked up a couple more trout nearly identical to the others, one a little larger, pushing thirteen inches. As the day wore on we began to see some bugs and finally some rising fish. Just above the ranch I saw what appeared to be a decent fish working below a riffle, but tight against the bank. So I camped on the spot and added some tippet material to my leader. The bugs were sparse and I couldn't tell what they were, so—what else when on the Boardman?—I tied on a small Adams, a fly that generations of anglers have used with success almost everywhere trout are found. The Adams was born on this very river in the 1920s, developed by local angler/tyer Len Halladay, who named it after an angling friend from Ohio. Little did he suspect back then that it would one day be famous on trout waters the world over.

I wasn't sure it would actually match what was hatching, but that of course is the beauty of the Adams. Besides, I wanted to fish with the fly on its home water.

At that moment Pete came by on the bank. "I see you have the juicier water again," he said.

"This little nothing of a riffle? I stopped here just so you could have that good pool right around the corner."

"I'm touched. But I don't suppose that fish over there that's sucking down flies every ten seconds had anything to do with it?"

"Is there something rising over there?" I said, shading my eyes. Like a machine, the fish rose again.

"If that's a five-inch brook trout *I'll* go get the beer," he said. "By the way, these cigars are very good."

"I'm glad you're enjoying them," I said. "I suppose you're going to stand there and watch?"

"Of course. I want to see you blow this one."

But it was too easy. A freshman at the Orvis school could have caught this trout. The fly landed a couple of feet upstream from the fish, rode a line of slick water, tumbled onto the eddy at the bottom, and was neatly snatched.

The trout bolted downstream and it was clear that this was a better fish. The river was shallow and the fish scampered everywhere, the light tippet slicing the water.

"There's still time to screw it up." This came from up on the bank.

Gradually the fish tired and I heard Pete slip into the river behind me. He was at my shoulder as I worked it in. It was another brown, a nice one, a couple of inches past the twelve-inch marker when laid against my rod. The small

Adams was snug in the corner of its mouth. I faced the trout upstream, letting the oxygen-rich riffle water pour through its gills. A minute later it shot away, leaving a long wake.

Pete stuck out his hand, a big smile on his face. "Nice fish, pal."

I was appropriately modest.

I then went way down, leaving Pete a series of good pools, all on tight bends with deeply undercut banks. I was ready to call it a day, particularly after that trout. But I continued to fish as I moved along and took a mixed bag of browns and brookies, mostly in the ten-inch class, all of them on the now scruffy-looking Adams. Finally, I came to the ranch, its long, broad lawn running down to the river's edge. I climbed out, propped my rod against a handy birch, slipped out of my vest and stretched. It had been a long but satisfying day.

I walked up to the lobby of the main building and inquired about a room. The kid behind the desk grinned when he saw me standing there in still-wet waders. I got the room key and went into the rustic bar, where I felt a lot less sillier, and bought a few cans of cold beer. "How'd you do?" the bartender asked.

Back down by the river, I sat on the bank, popped a beer open, and relaxed. It felt good to get the wader suspenders off the shoulders.

Presently Pete came around the bend upstream, reeled in, and lit the afterburner when he saw what I had. I never saw a guy in waders go that fast in the water. I handed him a cold one and he drained it. "That was the best beer I've ever tasted," he said with a belch.

We freshened up in the room, retrieved the car, and headed for the bar. Over cocktails, we discussed the day. Pete had also taken several more fish on dry flies, and a nice one to boot. He'd seduced them with Bivisibles, or so he said, a fly I've never fished and probably never will. But he likes the damned thing. ("It has class. Class and it works," he claims. Class? It's a brown and white fuzz ball.) At any rate, we both agreed that the Boardman had given us a good day, good at least for that stretch of it. Streamers in the morning, some satisfying dry-fly fishing in the afternoon. No outsized fish, but we didn't expect any. Just some classic fly fishing.

We were pooped and hungry and left the bar and found a table. The restaurant was nearly full. Most were out-of-state tourist types—"fudgies," as they're called. They had that look. (There are nearly as many fudge shops in northern Michigan as there are pine trees.) There was a group on the patio clustered around a big, half-barrel barbecue. Whatever was getting scorched smelled pretty damned good.

A chipper little waitress came over and handed us menus. I drained what remained of the martini I had carried over from the bar and ordered another one.

I didn't have to look at the menu. I knew that a dude ranch—even a midwestern version—would have a stockpile of steak in the kitchen. A couple of different kinds, as it turned out, and I ordered the biggest cut. So did Pete. Our waitress leveled with us and said the kitchen was a little backed up so it might be awhile, but she could bring our salads. I said fine and she looked at Pete. His eyes were closed.

"Sir?" she said.

Pete jerked awake.

"She wants to know if you want your salad now?" I said.

"Yeah, sure." His eyes fluttered. I said I was going to go out on the patio for a few minutes—I'd watch for the salad delivery. The waitress said fine; Pete mumbled something.

The group around the grill turned out to be a congress of adult Boy Scout leaders. There was much talk of merit badge training and so forth. My martini was the focus of so much lip-smacking attention I thought the glass was going to melt. I stood near a corner of the patio and watched a guy fish one of the ranch ponds stocked with rainbow trout that you can see but not catch. I have fished for them with grasshopper patterns (the grounds are alive with them at times) all the way down to Tricos on 7X. If the ranch ever becomes famous, it will be for a strain of rainbow trout that do not eat.

Turning, and peering through the window, I could see Pete, chin on his chest, eyes closed.

A guy sidled up to me and said quietly, "If I slip you ten bucks would you get me a double one of those—pointing at my drink—and take it around to the front of the building?"

I said sure, but there was the bar just ten feet away through the open door. I was curious—why didn't he just hop in there and get his own?

"Because some of the organizers of this little shindig are from Baptist churches, and they have a real thing about certain types of refreshment. I've got a flask stashed in my tent for a quiet little nightcap later. These guys are okay, but a Saturday night cookout without a see-through is un-American."

I was glad to do my good deed for the day, and as I maneuvered through the dining room I discovered that salads had been delivered to our table. Pete was sleeping, sitting up with his arms crossed on his chest.

I carried that big wet silver bullet through the lobby, thrilled to be part of a clandestine operation. It added a little extra excitement to an already outstanding day. Out front I found my panting scoutmaster.

"You get the Citizenship merit badge!" he exclaimed as we introduced ourselves.

"I already got it thirty years ago."

"Good for you. Then I'll put you in for an Oak Leaf Cluster or something," he said between sips. "And here, take these." He handed me a film canister. Inside were half a dozen of the prettiest Hendricksons I had ever seen. "I saw you get out of the river. I've been staring at these all day. I was hoping to get in some fishing myself. I tied 'em," he said modestly.

I thanked him, wished him luck, and back in the dining room gave Pete a shake. There was barely a response and I could tell that the lad was about done for. But I thought he wanted to eat, so I gave him another shake. This time his head came up and he looked at me through half-closed eyes. "Pete, there's your salad," I said.

"Rest my eyes for a minute," he mumbled. In an instant he was breathing deeply, his chin in his chest once again. I went to work on my salad, while I examined in more detail the fortuitously acquired Hendricksons, which now sat perkily on the tabletop. Our thirsty scoutmaster was, indeed, a lovely tyer.

The waitress came by with a basket of bread and gave Pete the eye. She looked at me with raised eyebrows. I smiled, my mouth full of salad. "Your steaks will be out in a minute," she said. "Should I bring his?" I nodded affirmatively.

Minutes later she was back. The entrées were truly beautiful, big and sizzling and just what the doctor ordered. I gave Pete a couple of good shakes—"Pete! Pete!"—and got no response except for a gentle snore.

I assaulted my steak, eating too fast, but luxuriating in every mouthful. I eyed Pete's, wondering.

And then suddenly, with a big sigh, Pete leaned forward, crossed his arms on the table around his plate, and rested the side of his face directly on that big, perfectly grilled porterhouse. A sixteen-ounce, medium-rare pillow. I kept eating, but with less enthusiasm because I could see that my chances for a double portion had diminished.

The waitress rushed over, horrified. "It's okay," I said. "He likes to sleep with his head on meat."

"Is he okay!?"

He was fine, I assured her. He was snoring steadily and attracting the attention of other diners, who were smiling and pointing, doubtless having never seen a man sleeping on his supper.

I helped myself to his side order of onion rings.

The snoring got a little louder and his exhalations were having an eroding effect on his vegetable selection. At regular intervals peas skipped off his plate and across the table. I thought about him possibly inhaling a couple and wondered if *that* would wake him. A little girl came by and stood and stared. People in the farther corners would stand and stretch for a look, smile or laugh, and sit back down.

I finished eating and thought about various ways of raising Pete's head to get at that steak—I'd slip the bread under there—but thought better as I recalled watching him smear himself with bug repellent a couple of times during the day. I couldn't imagine that Deep Woods Off would improve a steak. The mother came and collected the little girl, but not before giving my fishing partner a good looking-over.

I ordered cognac, two of them, in case Pete came around. But he didn't, so I was forced to drink his.

Finally, I started to get a little tuckered. I signed the check, left a tip, and after many minutes of prodding was able to partially rouse the sleeping beauty. In a daze he put an arm over my shoulder and I guided him out of the dining room—to a smattering of applause—and ultimately to our room, where he collapsed onto his bed. I removed his shoes, and that's all I remembered until the next morning.

I wakened to hear water running in the bathroom. Pete came out, pointed to his face, and asked, "How did I get these crosshatch marks on my cheek?"

5

❖

The Master of
Frenchman's Pond

Many years ago I quit the ad game for a time to own
and operate a fly fishing shop in a Detroit suburb. A couple
of months after the grand opening I received a letter post-
marked from a small town in the western Upper Peninsula.
The writer wanted to know if I had any 7X tippet material,
and if so, would I send several spools along with a bill. Indeed, I had plenty of 7X, and sent some up to John D. Voelker
in Ishpeming, Michigan.

A few days later another letter arrived from
Ishpeming. I recognized it immediately because it was addressed in the same green felt-tip pen, the handwriting sort
of sprawling and distinguished. Inside was a check for the
tippet material and a note with an editorial comment about
the eastern firm whose merchandise I was mostly carrying
in my shop. He mentioned something about two books he
had scribbled under the pen name "Traver" and then: "...the
bastards left both of them out of their current catalog."

I remember looking over at my little book department and seeing copies of *Trout Magic* and *Trout Madness*
on the shelves against the one wall, looking again at the note,
and putting two and two together.

The store was ahead of its time and remained open
for just two short years. But for nearly twenty years the

envelopes addressed with the green felt-tip pen kept coming. John Voelker—aka Robert Traver—thought that two great American art forms were on the decline: good letter writing and good storytelling. He told a great yarn and wrote an even better letter. The letters come no more. John Voelker died on March 10, 1991, at the age of eighty-seven. He had a heart attack in his Jeep on a U.P. back road during a trip to the post office.

I learned of his passing the next day, and that evening I rummaged around in a kitchen cupboard for a certain jelly jar, and in it mixed an industrial-strength bourbon old-fashioned and sat on my patio in the dark.

For many years at Voelker's fishing camp the bourbon old-fashioned was the official camp drink, and at four o'clock every afternoon the fishing stopped and a round was poured. They were almost always made in the big jelly jars and it didn't take many drinks to kill a fifth. These particular jelly jars were hard to find and John was always on the lookout for them.

One afternoon, several seasons ago, when the fishing at camp was lousy, John and I set off on a "prowl" (as he called them) along two-trackers in the woods and took our drinks with us. We bumped along, slopping whiskey on us, allegedly looking for some ancient stone building. Actually it was just an excuse for a ramble in the woods. We found no mysterious structure, but had a great time anyway.

At the end of the expedition John dropped me at my truck. I still had half a drink left. It was a long drive out of the woods and I said that I was going to take my drink with me. John looked pained and I knew why.

"Don't worry. I'll bring back the glass the next time I'm here."

"You're sure?"

"Yes."

"You won't forget?"

"No."

He was looking at the glass as though he was witnessing the kidnapping of his wife and daughters.

"I'll wash it, of course."

"I would have assumed that."

"I won't let you down."

"He said to his probation officer."

He ambled toward his Jeep. "I know I can count on you, lad." I knew that some fun was at hand. It was exactly this sort of innocent gamesmanship that he liked, and the glass became the point of wonderful sparring, both at camp and in the mail. From a letter, written sideways in the margin: "Headline! Ex-Judgie Comes Out of Retirement—Issues Warrant For Jelly Jar Thief!"

Of course the glass never made it back to camp. That would have ended the fun. Eventually, somehow, somewhere, my father found a whole case of exactly those particular jars and shipped them off to the U.P. From a letter: "Your old man shipped me an entire case of bourbon glasses which earns him the combination to the gate and the undying gratitude of the regulars out at camp."

So I sat in the dark on my patio, glass in hand, and thought about my old pal. The wind, as it often is in northern Michigan, was crisp and sharp and reminded me of Voelker's affinity for the weather. And then a wedge of geese landed on Boardman Lake and I thought about how he loved all things wild, particularly his remote corner of the Upper Peninsula.

He was an attorney in private practice, a prosecuting attorney, and a Michigan Supreme Court justice. Along the way he wrote eleven books including his three trout fishing things: *Trout Magic, Trout Madness,* and *Anatomy of a Fisherman. Trout Madness* is arguably one of the best collections of trout fishing yarns ever written. His big commercial success came in 1958 with *Anatomy of a Murder.* It was a bestseller, and Otto Preminger made it into a film starring Jimmy Stewart, George C. Scott, Lee Remick, and

Ben Gazzarra. Voelker took the money and ran straight from Lansing back to the Upper Peninsula. He loved the law and was proud to have served on the state's highest court. But he loved the wild U.P. even more. It was where he was born, raised, practiced law, and from about 1960 onward lived the Life of Riley, in the eyes of his fishing pals.

With part of the proceeds from the sale of the movie rights, Voelker bought the land surrounding an ancient beaver pond where he had been fishing for many years. It is actually more like a long, narrow lake. The original beavers had dammed the creek in a narrows between two bluffs, creating a picture-book pond. From time to time Voelker reinforced the dam. Unlike many old beaver ponds, this one sustained a relatively healthy population of wild brook trout, probably because the fish had access to spawning gravel in what remained of the creek upstream.

Over the years a camp grew on the granite shelf near the center, narrow part of the pond. First a cabin—"the shack"—followed by a shed and footbridge over the narrows. A brick barbecue was the Bicentennial Year project. Then there were the "accessories," for one of the proprietor's favorite pastimes was roaming the U.P. and poking around at yard sales and flea markets. Whatever he found ended up in camp. Bird cages with papier-mâché residents hung from trees. Pots and pans hung from trees, shed walls, and covered one side of the shack. Buckets and vases were everywhere: on the ground, on crates, on tables, most of them filled with bunches of dried wild grass. Green telephone pole glass insulators adorned a shelf nailed to a jack pine. Signs. Signs everywhere. "Tavern" (at least four or five), "Home of the U.P. Cribbage Champ," "Caution— Chipmunk Crossing" (on the bridge), "Home of the *Former* U.P. Cribbage Champ," "Spare the Hill, Brake Gently!" "Blatz." Furniture: stools, rocking chairs, benches, and church pews placed just so for pond viewing, some of this stuff older than the owner. And my favorite, the refrigerator that stood next to the shack, miles from the nearest electricity. ("Where would judgie plug it in?" he would mutter, followed by, "My, my.")

The inside of the shack was much the same, but with some semblance of order. On the far wall, on either side of the little potbelly stove, were shelves with canned goods to one side and the infamous jelly jars and assorted tableware on the other. There was a small couch against another wall and a round table in the corner. The master's chair was next

to the door where he could look out the window and see the pond. ("In case I see a mermaid.") There was not a single square inch of the interior of the shack that wasn't covered with something: old calendars, faded dust jackets from his books, objects and gadgets that admirers had carved or made and had sent him. Baskets hung from the ceiling, filled with odds and ends. He had a battery-powered radio on the window ledge next to his chair. The radio had a short antenna with an alligator clip. He could attach the clip to another antenna that ran up the side of the shack and over to a nearby jack pine. With this rig he could pick up classical music that originated at the famous music camp at Interlochen in the northern Lower Peninsula.

He called the place "Frenchman's Pond," and for three decades, early spring through late fall, not many days passed that the master wasn't at his playground.

His search for 7X tippet material led to an exchange of correspondence that grew livelier and friendlier and then one day he wrote, "If you're up this way raise a smoke signal."

As it turned out, Pete Treboldi and I were headed for a week of fishing in the U.P. a month or so later. We made arrangements to rendezvous with Voelker in the parking lot of a bar not far from the side road that eventually led back to his camp. Pete and I were seven minutes late and Voelker was nowhere in sight. Actually, he was sitting in his Jeep—one of the old Willys—in the woods nearby, checking us out. When he emerged, we had a friendly, but rather formal conversation and then followed him for a couple of miles through the woods until the trail became impassable for a city car. He stopped the old Jeep, motioned us over, and we had another powwow. This time the conversation was a little strained. Then Pete came up with a box of Italian cigars and I hauled out some tippet material and a few flies I had pilfered from the store. His mood brightened considerably and he finally made room for our gear in the old Jeep and back to camp we went. He had just hauled in a load of gravel to fill in ruts on the trail as it descends the hill into camp. Pete and I spent more than an hour, stripped to the waist, shoveling gravel down the hill, John barking directions. There were trout rising all over the pond, and about the time Pete and I got near the bottom of that pile of gravel, the rise was so good the old guy called a halt and everyone charged for their fly rods.

At four o'clock that day I drank my first bourbon old-fashioned in the shack and began a friendship that lasted until his passing. Along with Pete and Harry Campbell, I would return to the pond time after time. John gave us the combination to the gate and told us where the keys to the shack and shed were hidden. The camp was ours to use whether he was there or not. I often visited alone, as did Harry, who had made Voelker's acquaintance while going to school at Northern Michigan University. An additional bonus was getting to know Ted Bogdan and Lloyd Anderson, two of John's pals. When I tried marriage for a second time and John was kind enough to host the ceremony out at camp, Ted, who owned the best restaurant in the U.P., catered a wonderful thing pondside and an equally great reception back at his joint later. Lloyd was kind enough to organize a convoy of four-wheel-drive vehicles to carry the wedding party through the woods.

In all the years I knew him I only had to write one difficult letter to John: the one telling him that the marriage had not worked out. His reply came immediately. It was exactly the right blend of sadness and wit, understanding and advice, and it raised my spirits considerably.

Love affairs with fly rods sometimes send us to some pretty nifty places; it's one of the bennies that comes with the sport. I've been lucky enough to have run after wolves on salmon rivers near the Arctic Circle and to have chased trout on unexplored mountain rivers in the rain forests of Central America. But my favorite place in the world was inside that shack at four o'clock after a day of fishing at the pond, or rambling around two-trackers in the woods with John.

We solved the world's problems, swapped stories, talked about politics, women, sex, booze, literature—any subject was fair game. There were of course endless fishing yarns, but often the talk would be about writing. There were magic moments, such as the time Harry leaned across the table and wondered if John knew that one of Harry's ancestors played a key role in a Traver novel.

John straightened, puzzled. I looked at Harry. The sun was just setting over the tops of the pines. Somewhere in the woods a white-throated sparrow sang his *Old-Sam-Peabody-Peabody-Peabody* song. I'll never forget that moment.

Very quietly Harry said, "My great-great-grandfather James Campbell was the Michigan justice who wrote the majority opinion in the case that became your *Laughing Whitefish*."

You could have heard a pin drop. It was the only time I've ever seen the old guy speechless. (It was absolutely true; John even put Justice Campbell in the book.)

Finally, "My God, a descendant of old Justice Campbell right here in my fishing shack. My, my, my."

It was a terribly poignant moment and John was extremely moved.

He had the mien of a supreme court justice and the wit of a vaudeville comedian. He loved a good time, good food, and good booze. He loved it when my late father, his pal "Reecher," would visit because my old man could drink with the best of them. ("I await you and Reecher on that date. Am exercising my liver for his arrival," he once wrote.)

Between visits there were the letters. Once, when I got lazy, I received a short, curt note: "Are you mad at me

Jamus? Report in!" He closed many letters with a phrase any pond fisherman would understand: "A cloud is passing over and I must run!"

From a letter, June 25th, 1985

Harry had already written me a hilarious account of his brush with a sneaky backwoods cop. The last time a cop stopped me I said 'Ossifer, I only had two nickel beers' so he took me in and grilled me for hours to find out where you could still find such a bargain in beer. I've got a yarn in the latest Rod an Reel that may give you a giggle. Run don't walk...

April 16, 1975,complaining that a certain eastern mail-order house wasn't carrying his books, just before the season opener.

Ten more days 'till the big parole, when Orvis can go pee up a tree.

June 26, 1982

Fishing has been slow, i.e., just plain lousy, (at the pond) tho Ted has landed some weight-lifter browns out on the beeg river. So I mostly explore back roads picking mushrooms, sighting flora and having fauna (ha,ha)...

June 28, 1983

I'll be 80 tomorrow, almost as traumatic as when I was 40—or "farty" as the Irish would say.

Letter to Harry, Oct. 5, 1983, referring to a calendar Harry had sent featuring a bare-bottomed gal modeling a raincoat

Thanks for the—uh—inspiring calendar, which I plan to paste on the ceiling over my bed until I can enlarge my shack. It must have taken a lot of cheek to produce a calendar like that—"Oh comely lass, with cheeks of tan; I'll lie on my ass, looking at yours..." (Rhyme a little weak, meter *a*shew!)

Letter to Harry, June 18, 1981

Much modern writing about fishing is getting as opaque and rarefied as footnoted criticism or essays on the orgasm; lots of talk, talk, talk but damn little fun to read.

January 22, 1983

With a heavy heart I turned down the Paul Young (T.U. Chapter) invite; too far to go at the wrong time; too little time to mix drinks *my* way; too many tattered old books to sign from Cheryl to Gary with love...

April 15, 1981

The shirts arrived but I still can't get Ted's boobiest waitress to model them for us. Many thanks. Harry's letter ought to be the lead article in the goddam magazine and maybe help muzzle the computer technicians who have moved into fly fishing. Actually, the bastards make fishing sound like an overtime session at the office to listen to a pep spiel from the head man—just what it *ain't*.

January 31, 1986, after a round of short notes about poetry, about which I contributed nothing

I stalled after the first line of this epic poem—"I'll never ever forget what's her name..."

Letter to Harry, May 9, 1985

Twenty frozen guys showed up of the Hypothermic Hopening Day and a wizened 10-incher won the prize. Ted cooked a stew and my wife did the macaroni and trimmings, so everyone got a little stewed. (I worked on that one.)

Letter to Harry, August 19, 1982, on missing each other on trips out to camp

Sorry we missed...though I found and enjoyed that distilled spoor you left!

November 9, 1976

Charles Kuralt flew in to wind up the last of the season. He and his crew did a thing here at Frenchman's several years ago during which he got badly hooked on fly fishing & this country. Naturally the fishing was lousy but we bravely drowned our blues in bourbon and charcoal steaks & he wants to come back. The day before he arrived I could have filled a barrel, but I only kept three, the prize going exactly 12 ½ inches, which he had for breakfast.

February 24, 1984, from a ramble about writing

...also proof that anything that reads easily, the writer must have worked his ass off to produce.

Letter to Harry, May 22, 1981, after Harry sent posters depicting mayflies, stone flies, etc...

My plan is to have pickets parade the pond with your posters—woops, I've run out of pees...

An undated letter covering many topics including the bees in camp

Nectar, hell he laid her!

January 3, 1975

There is only one Voelker Lake that I know of and, yes, it is indeed the scene of The Little Panama spasm. On some maps there is also a Voelker Creek (also after me old man) that flows into Silver Lake, but is miles away from Voelker Lake.

June 11, 1980

Sorry I missed you, but thanks for the 10X...which causes a lot of eyeraising among my fishing pals. I used some the other day and on the third cast a slob rose and grabbed not the fly but the leader and then, lo, rose once again, smacking his lips and shading his eyes and hollered at me "Man, what's her phone number?"

❖

And so throughout the years they came. When I learned of his passing I knew that I would miss receiving those green scrawled letters as much as anything. I drove up to Ishpeming for the funeral services to pay my last respects. On the day after the visitation, family and friends gathered and simply talked about what he had meant to us all. There was no preaching, and many of the remembrances were funny, which is just the way he would have liked it.

It was a sad trip back from the U.P., but my hair nearly stood on end when I arrived home and checked my mail. There in the box was an envelope with the familiar handwriting, but the ink was a melancholy dark blue. I mixed a stiff drink, opened the envelope, and read the letter. He had written and mailed it the day he died.

"Dear Jim, I've 'ad even more eye surgery—this time a new lens—so I haven't done much writing or reading including your piece in the recent *Esquire*. I'm sorry you're again caught in the toils of urban living, though I recall that a long prowl I once made of Traverse City was a beauty—up to some far point or other and back another way…lovely.

"Snowshoers report that the old camp is still there and the pond and the bridge. But the trout aren't there like they used to be when we used to watch them rise like ticking clocks. Come up when you can old friend. Best, John."

6

THE TRUE STORY
OF THE DANCING FLY

Northern Michigan is capable of days so perfect that only an idiot would fail to sense the wonderment. The air has an almost crystal feel to it, a clarity that seems to have a knifelike edge.

Personally, I think it has something to do with Lake Superior, the big inland sea just to the north of us. I also think it has something to do with all the iron in the ground. Somehow I think the iron energizes the air and gives it that something I can't describe. I don't even want to know if my theory is geologically possible; I just prefer to believe it. You may laugh if you like. John Voelker and I were in accord on this. When the U.P. handed over such a day it was sometimes better to sit in the sun in camp and wonder over it. It was a day for sitting around on the church pews he had hauled into his fishing camp—Frenchman's Pond—and speculate on things that seemed to need speculating about. Besides, the shy, wild brook trout in Frenchman's were tough when it was bright.

On this particular day—one of those special ones— John was a little annoyed. Earlier in the day he had been moved to comment on the particularly pretty bird song he had heard coming from the woods up behind the shack.

"Why would you be upset about something like that?" I asked.

"Lloyd told me it was a damned sparrow making that song." Lloyd was one of John's old-time fishing buddies. John suggested we listen.

It wasn't a minute before a white-throated sparrow sang. If you've heard one you know it for its unique cadence that sounds like *Old-Sam-Peabody-Peabody-Peabody*.

"Is that it?" I asked.

"That's it," John said.

"Well, I hate to disappoint you."

"I can see you're already siding with Lloyd."

Pete Treboldi had gone to our car for a box of cigars and was now coming back down the hill.

"Yer honor..." I began.

"Tank you, tank you," he replied with a bob of his head. (He didn't much like to be called "Judge" although he often referred to himself in the third person as "Judgie," but I would occasionally toss out a "yer honor," which I secretly knew he got a kick out of, in deference to his years on the Michigan Supreme Court.)

"I think we have a semi-expert witness here," I continued. "Pete generally knows a robin from a heron. Let's see what he says."

Pete passed out cigars and we asked him to listen. Sure enough, Old Sam Peabody trilled again.

"Oh, that's that little sparrow, what the hell's the name of it?"

"Damn!" said John. "At least tell me they're found only in the U.P."

"Well, not really," I said.

"Damn!"

He was standing now, assuming sort of a courtroom pose.

"For decades, lads, I've thought that song belonged to some exotic bird I never saw. It was always around the next bend in the trail or just over the next hill, too beautiful for words! For fifty years at least I've been waiting to stumble on this beauty. And now it turns out to be a damned sparrow!"

Then he began to chuckle. "With a little luck I'll be able to go on."

We sat in the sun next to the long, narrow pond. Way up a trout rose. Chipmunks scurried around our feet.

The talk got around to writing, as it often did. We talked about some of the people and places in the U.P. that ended up as the basis for his books and stories. His two best novels, *Anatomy of a Murder* and *Laughing Whitefish,* were based on actual court cases, both in the U.P. Upper Peninsula characters also populated his two collections of trout yarns, *Trout Madness* and *Trout Magic.*

"Did you ever just plain make a story up, a complete and total fabrication?" I asked.

He sat bolt upright and looked at me as though he'd seen a ghost.

I was startled, too, and wondered if I had said something that offended him. He stood and ambled over to the ice chest on the picnic table next to the shack and got a beer. He returned, popped the tab, and took a long pull.

"Everything I've written has had some basis in fact—almost," he said. "I did fabricate one yarn that had no basis in fact and it's always bothered me."

I found myself in the ridiculous position of explaining to a respected author of many works that, essentially, anything goes in fiction. Pete looked amused.

"That's not what I mean, lads. What bothers me is that I don't really know if what I wrote about would really work."

Pete and I exchanged glances.

"But today we're going to find out!" he exclaimed.

Off he went again, this time to the shed. Pete and I watched as he rooted around. "Jamus, Pete! Come here lads!"

Pete and I scurried to the shed. John had a ball of string and two long cane poles. "We're going to need about three feet of tippet. Who has a spool of 5X?"

Pete produced the tippet material and we followed John down to the pond.

"This will be a day to remember, I guarantee it lads!"

John handed me one of the cane poles and told me to go around to the opposite side of the pond, which I did, sharing the bridge over the pond's narrow center with a couple of chipmunks. Finally I reached a casting platform opposite John and Pete, cane pole in hand. It was long, ten or twelve feet.

I thought back over John's stories and I couldn't make a cane pole connection. John and Pete seemed to be very busy with the ball of string, Pete's cane pole, the spool of tippet material, and various fly boxes. I could see John very carefully coiling string in a pile on the ground.

"Stand by, Jamus!" hollered John.

I watched as Pete tied the string to a heavy stick, reared back and threw it in my direction. The pond is not wide anywhere and the stick arced nicely over the pond and landed nearby in the brush at my side.

"Al Kaline couldn't have done it better!" John was full of directions now. "Jamus! Tie the string to the end of your cane pole! Be quick lad! Pete, stand by to take up slack!"

A minute later I had the string tied to the end of my cane pole. Pete started taking up slack on his end and moments later the string hung suspended over Frenchman's Pond. Near the center of the string was a dropper. I could see a small dry fly at its end.

And then it came to me. "The Dancing Fly" in *Trout Magic*. Timmy and Pinky.

"Okay lads. Wiggle your poles so that the fly dances up and down on the surface of the pond." He was fairly cackling now.

"What do we do if we get one?" Pete asked.

"What do you mean *if,* said John, pretending to be shocked. "It's just a matter of time. Could be any moment!"

I had the notion that perhaps history was being made this day at Frenchman's Pond and I think Pete sensed the same thing. Between wisecracks we worked hard to develop a rhythm, which proved to be difficult. Sometimes the fly jumped eight or ten feet in the air and never came near the surface; sometimes the string hit the water with a splat. When that happened, John turned away with a grimace.

Finally Pete figured out that if one of us remained motionless, the other guy could make the fly dance. And dance it did. Pete and I took turns. John looked pleased.

In his story "The Dancing Fly," John writes as the character Al, and fishes the pond with his two buddies, Pinky and Timmy. They all notice a small fly that dances over the pond's surface during their first visit and no one has a pattern, much less a technique, that will work. Al tracks down an entomology professor in a distant New England town who not only identifies the bug, but ties some up.

Naturally, Al, Timmy, and Pinky are betting men, and Al cleans house with his new, secret pattern. Toward the end of that season Timmy and Pinky grow weary of emptying their wallets. One day, when Al is out of sight on the lower part of the pond, Pinky and Timmy fish the upper pond with their new technique and score big-time. Naturally, Al catches them and in the end...whoops!

"Are you happy now?" I yelled across the pond.

"I'm very pleased. I can see where this might actually work. I'll be ecstatic, however, when you lads catch one. Keep at it fellas, I'm going for a drink."

Pete and I heard the cabin door open, then the tinkle of ice cubes, then a barely perceptible chuckle, maybe even some laughter. I looked at Pete. Pete looked at me. We both looked at our bobbing cane poles and the silly dancing fly. Then I started to giggle and Pete burst out laughing. I swore

I heard more laughter from the cabin. We were both laughing like hell as I reached up with my snippers and cut the string at the tip of my pole.

John was already making old-fashioneds when Pete and I entered the shack. "Any luck lads?"

"What do you think," Pete said.

"My, my, my, I do feel better," he said with a smirk.

❖

Inside the shack, to the left of the door as you entered, was a small, round table. It was just large enough to accommodate two chairs. The chair by the door was always John's. There, under the windowsill, he kept a yellow pad, a smaller version of a yellow legal pad.

On the surface, the pad appeared to be nothing more than a way to list camp chores. There were always chores out at Frenchman's. The list might read, for example:

1. Haul planks to other side
2. Sunflower seeds for chipmunks
3. Repair casting platform at top log
4. Get butter beans (He liked to eat them, unheated, out of the can.)

There might be a couple of things crossed off, but there always seemed to be things that needed doing. Naturally, as a guest, you tried to help out, even when he wasn't there. Once, at the top of the list, my brother-in-law, Ron "Olive Matuka" Randlett, and I found, "Move woodpile away from cabin door."

Sure enough, he had hauled in a load of slab wood with his trailer and dumped it too close to the cabin door. If you disturbed the pile, you got a cascade of wood right onto the doorstep. Here was a chore that clearly needed doing. Ron and I checked the pond. There were no risers. So we stripped to the waist and threw slab wood over what remained of the old pile. That way the seasoned stuff would be closest to the door.

It was a large pile, but with both of us working we had it rearranged in an hour or so. In fact, we finished just as a hatch of midges came off and the brook trout began to rise. I crossed the chore off the list and Ron and I went fishing.

A few days later, at home near Detroit (I had not yet found my way north for good) I received a letter that read, in part:

"Imagine my surprise at arriving at camp on Monday to discover that somehow the woodpile got moved and I am no longer in danger of being buried in a wooden avalanche as I enter and exit the shack. It will remain a mystery! You and Ron are welcome back anytime! But you know that. Very mysterious—perhaps a mermaid moved the woodpile?"

To him the pond was a special place and he liked to know that others thought so, too. To that end, the yellow pads served another purpose.

He often left the pages of the yellow pads intact as the pads filled. Rather than rip off pages, he simply flipped them over. Interspersed among the list of chores were notes from those who had fished the pond, especially in the evening after John had left. (He stayed through the cocktail hour, but most often left to have dinner at home.) These reports were almost always about the evening's fishing, but many went beyond that. There, in the pages of these often moldy pads of paper, were wonderful tributes to the pond.

I used to wonder if the pond affected others as it affected me. You almost felt as though you were reading someone else's mail as you flipped through the pad, but you couldn't stop. Others knew the magic of the place and felt as I did. And the writing was wonderful. It was sweet prose written at the moment by people who were deeply moved. Sometimes you would find a poem, written by Indian Jim, a native American and a pal of John's.

The yellow pads became a link between the man and his place, his friends and his trout. A pad would disappear to be replaced with a new one, and I wonder still if he saved them and read through them to remember distant friends and how they felt the magic of the place, as he did.

❖

I once visited the pond with a woman I then loved and John was much taken with her. She was a fly fishing novice and John went out of his way to be a perfect and charming host and nicknamed her Miss Boardwalk after one of the casting platforms.

She, in turn, adored John, and not long after we returned home she mailed him a small, round, many-faceted prism as a thank-you.

John hung the prism in the window of the shack on a short length of tippet material. When the sun was just right, he would give it a little flick with his finger and set it spinning. Sunlight, in all the colors of the rainbow, would dance about the cabin. He loved that prism, and every summer I would take it down and shine it up.

Over the years my special friend would come to fly fishing in a big way, and our paths would cross and recross. We drifted in and out of each other's lives; two adventurers with eyes on far horizons.

She never returned to the pond and John often asked about her and my answer was always the same: either I was free and she was committed to something, or she was free and I was involved. Our timing left a lot to be desired.

When I was involved I would sometimes take the person of the moment to the pond knowing what was going to happen at the four o'clock cocktail hour, especially if the sun was shining. John would go through the ritual of preparing bourbon old-fashioneds. My companion's eyes would be roaming the shack, for the inside was something to behold. John would serve the old-fashioneds and would begin eyeing the prism. I would give him a little kick under the table. He would smirk. I would try to divert his attention, which never worked. Inevitably, he would say something like "isn't the sunlight pretty coming through the window." I would give him a pretty solid boot. And then it would happen. Very casually, with his left hand, he would reach up and spin the prism and then take a quick drink. I would give him a real good whack under the table and he would feign pain.

Naturally, my companion would be fascinated by the spinning prism with its light show. And since John had spent a good part of the day showing my friend around camp, pointing out all the stuff he had hauled in over the years, along with a little story about where he found everything, it was only natural that the prism had a story too.

"Let me see. How *did* I get that?" he would respond to the question that always leapt from pretty lips. Sure as hell, I knew what was coming and it always came with the biggest smirk: "Jamus, help me out. Do you recall how I got this lovely prism?"

"I have no idea, John," I would lie through my teeth.

And then he'd have me and off he'd go, never quite getting to the answer, but never quite letting me off the hook. While the evidence merrily spun, I squirmed. It was courtroom drama at its best.

Whenever I was in camp with a woman, John always left after a cocktail or two. "You two kids can have the run of the place," he would say, pretending to do me a huge favor.

The minute the door of his Jeep would slam shut and the engine would start it would come; you could bet the family dog on it. "All right, what's the deal with the prism?"

Finally there was the long-ago day that I got married at Frenchman's. It was a blustery October day with a stiff wind off Lake Superior to the north. It rained a little and some of the wedding party took to the shack, including me and my about-to-be in-laws. John began to mix drinks, all puffed up over the elegant flower someone had pinned to his sweater. He was, of course, on center stage and loving every minute of it. Suddenly, there was a break in the clouds. A shaft of sunlight burst through the window. John stopped mixing and looked at me with just a hint of a smile. I shook my head ever so slightly. He began to fuss with the drinks again. And ever so casually reached up and gave that little prism a modest spin.

It was my about-to-be mother-in-law who had to ask about the prism. The smirk was bigger than usual, but he very skillfully changed the subject.

There was a knothole in a jack pine near the edge of the pond. He would ask first-time visitors to the pond if they'd seen any trout rising. If the answer was no, he'd say "watch this" and stick his finger in the knothole as though he were pushing a button. A moment later he would point up the pond and, sure enough, rings would be spreading across the water.

"My, my," he would say with a chuckle.

7

❖

THE GURGLE OF
GREAT EXPECTATIONS

For a while I had a dog, a big, handsome German shorthair whose mission in life was to bring me my boots. That
was the first job I taught him, believing that any dog ought
to be as useful as possible during the off-season. Casey Jones
was a boot-fetching machine and would often bring my everyday boots without my asking for them. I would look up
from my desk and there he would be, statue-still in the hall-
way, front paw raised, head cocked, with a big leather boot
in his mouth.

He learned other jobs, such as fetching my pipe, as
long as it didn't have coals in it, which he found distasteful.
About the time he had his first birthday he was responding
to hand signals and I could get him to bring me just about
anything he could get in his mouth by saying "That's it!"
when he reached the object I wanted.

Like most dogs he had a few bad habits. I had trouble
keeping him off beds, but it was hard to get worked up about
that because for the first three months he was with me he
slept in mine, under the covers. At the time I was living in a
farmhouse that only had heat in the kitchen. That winter it
often got down to zero or so in the bedrooms, and the only
way to keep him from freezing was to have him under the

covers with me. A year later, when he weighed sixty pounds, he still thought his rightful place was under the covers next to me.

I had been years without a dog, and when I left the apartment in the city for northern Michigan, a furry companion was a priority. Like all bird hunters musing over a litter of candidates, my selection process was strictly scientific. He crawled out of the pile and licked my hand. That was that. He was also mostly white. He had a liver-colored head with a white star and flecked muzzle and a solid liver patch on his right rear leg. Other than that, his base coat was white with an even distribution of light liver flecking. There was some speculation that the flecking would fill in as he matured, but it never did. He was a snap to see when the ferns started to turn from green to brown not long after the season opened. He stood out in the dismal brown ferns like a lighthouse.

Having Casey Jones was an extra incentive to jump in the truck and explore two-trackers on days when I couldn't rustle up a trout guiding gig. Getting lost on two-trackers is one way to have a lot of fun, and there are a lot of them in northern Michigan. With the dog, exploration took on a new purpose. Now I could eyeball places to hunt that I would have passed up before the acquisition of Super Nose.

One day the two of us were deep within a wild place adjacent to a stream whose banks for many miles are cabin-free. This is a vast area thick with stands of aspen of all sizes, interlaced between forests of red, white, and jack pine. There are a lot of little creeks and the closer you get to the river the wilder the terrain gets. Those who fish the river come in from the opposite side because a very genteel dirt road runs near it for some distance. Since the mission was grouse coverts, I was on the side I much preferred. Give me ridges and valleys and swamps and mysterious little coldwater creeks running beneath tangles of cedar.

I was following the compass mounted on the dash-board, trying to put together a network of two-trackers that would take me through thick stands of aspen in a generally south-to-north direction. It was late September and the afternoon air was clear and had that certain sharpness about it. There were already touches of red where interloping maples showed some color.

I was bumping along at a crawl when, looking over my shoulder, I noticed that Casey Jones was not in the back of the pickup. I kept him in the cab on the highway, but once in the woods he rode in back. He enjoyed the scenery and the fresh air and I had the seat dog-free so I could spread out topographic maps.

So I stopped and turned off the engine and got out of the truck, trying to figure out a nonviolent way to teach sixty pounds of puppy that jumping ship without permission is a no-no.

I knew he had to be somewhere close because he'd been in the truck only moments before. So I sauntered down the two-tracker aways and, sure enough, spotted a flash of white up in an open grove of aspen. It was goofball all right, and he took my breath away because he was locked in a picture-perfect point, rock-solid, head down, one foreleg in the air. A textbook point.

Now the act of abandoning ship without permission took on another dimension. I quickly lost interest in disciplinary activities. I had visions of a covert lousy with grouse. What else would have made my ordinarily well-behaved Casey Jones jump out of the truck? So I chose the middle ground. If, indeed, he'd found the mother lode of grouse, he'd get no biscuit as a reward. But he also wouldn't get punished when we got back to the truck. If this was a false point, we'd have a stern talk and he would ride in the cab with his window closed.

I watched as he broke point and crept forward and locked on point again. I quietly moved in behind him, and as he became aware that I was there his stub of a tail wiggled slightly. I must say he was a sight.

He started to creep forward again and I gave him a whispered "no" while I tried to figure out how a platoon of grouse could hide so well. The drama ended when, a moment later, a troop of turkeys flushed with a roar some distance in front of us. I grabbed his collar and stroked his sides to settle him down. He had never come up against turkeys and he was jelly.

While I was getting him settled I became aware of a sound that, once you've heard it and sampled its implications, can actually make you forget sex for more than half an hour. It was the sound of water moving through a beaver dam. It was off to my right and I could see an opening in the trees and then a few pines half-dead for no apparent reason; the dead giveaway. How did I know it was water moving through a beaver dam? I don't know. I just knew. Sure, it could have been water going over a log. But it had that certain forced gurgle to it. The gurgle of great expectations.

Turkeys forgotten, the pooch and I followed our ears and not two minutes later descended a small hill into a clearing and, bingo, there it was. A picture-perfect beaver pond, somewhat on the smallish side but, judging by the cuttings, relatively new. My heart raced when, out in the middle, a trout rose. And then another. Just those two. But that didn't matter. The pond was in full sun and there wasn't a cloud in the sky. Beaver pond trout are much spookier than their cousins that live in moving water, and a bright day often keeps them hidden.

I gave a little whoop and said a prayer to the trout gods and got very generous in the dog biscuit department. I later determined the name of the creek the beavers had dammed, but right then I didn't know where I was. All I knew is that I had added a new pond to my inventory. We explored the perimeter of the pond looking for signs of other human visitors, particularly the most depressing sign of all, the empty cottage cheese container. But the joint was in pristine shape.

The dam was about twenty yards across, with an interesting-looking little pool at its base in which I saw something flash. The creek itself was maybe three yards wide, a jewel of a thing that disappeared where a little meadow ended and the jungle began again. I could see that exploring downstream would be work.

There were fresh mud and cuttings on the dam and the beaver lodge itself appeared to be against the south shore of the pond. Contrary to what many people think, beavers don't always build their hotels in the center of their ponds.

Naturally, goofball had to try to cross the dam and fell in on the upstream side when he was halfway across. He scratched the hell out of his belly trying to get back on the

dam, falling immediately again on the downstream side. Beaver dams, especially new ones, are very difficult to walk on, particularly if you have four legs to worry about. Anyway, all this was great entertainment to me and actually helpful because I saw several flashes here and there around the dam as C. J. did his half gainers. The pond was full of trout.

The most important thing about finding a new beaver pond is finding your way back to it. That sounds silly, but a remote pond full of brookies with no sign of human visitors isn't that way because it's easy to find. As much as I wanted to fish the pond that day, especially with the trout season drawing to a close, there was another priority. I whistled up the wet pooch, put him in the back of the pickup, and backtracked. At each fork in the two-track I got out of the truck and cut a small blaze mark at the base of an aspen. I always put the mark on the opposite side I needed to take when I got to that fork in the trail. In other words, if I needed to take the right fork, I put a mark at the base of a tree (never eye level) on the left side of the trail. That way, obviously, anyone curious enough to notice and follow the marks would go the wrong way. Hopefully. The only time the system gets complicated is when I have to put two marks at the base of a tree. That means there's something good in both directions. The only dangerous time is the first week or so when the marks are fresh. They weather fast and I don't cut many of them.

An hour or so of backtracking with just one wrong turn and I had the route marked well enough to find my way back again. I prayed to the god of beaver ponds that no one would come along and discover my special prize. It is rare that you can drive so close to them.

The second most important thing about finding a new beaver pond is to never tell anyone about it. Not anyone. I have violated Rule II a couple of times, but only with my best friends, Pete and Maz. They're too smart to ruin a good thing.

No, in my part of Michigan, finding a beaver pond loaded with trout is like finding Elle McPherson naked in your bed. Sharing isn't in the cards.

So here I was—a few weeks into the bird season with a brand new bird dog and a brand new beaver pond. And trout season was only a few days from closing. It's stuff like this that makes your hair turn gray.

Each morning I woke to sixty pounds of German shorthair staring me in the face, rock-solid next to the bed, hope oozing from every pore in his body. On the opening day of grouse and woodcock season he had discovered the real reason for his existence. Naturally, he thought we would do this wonderful new thing every day. And we did, at least on those days I didn't have a guiding job. I loved him because he was not a whiner. Instead, he'd stand or sit with his head cocked and vibrate with expectation. Sometimes I wished he would race around and bark and let it all hang out, but that wasn't his style.

Two mornings in a row, after the discovery of the pond, I gave in to the beautiful, beady yellow eyes and we grabbed the 28-gauge, lunch, and a thermos of coffee and off we went. But that damned pond was on my mind. I rationalized that it would be there in the spring, but right then spring was several centuries in the future. It took the Egyptians less time to build the Great Pyramids than it takes to go from autumn to spring in northern Michigan.

On the third morning following the discovery of the pond—and the last day of trout season—the phone rang as I was making coffee and congratulating myself on a momentous decision. I had decided I would give up a half day of bird hunting with my new ace in order to fish the pond in the afternoon. But wouldn't you know it. There on the phone was one of the fly shops for which I worked and they had a walk-in who wanted a guide for the last day.

This had not been in the plans. I panicked and there was a rush of indecision. I really needed the work, but I had my heart set on a visit to the pond, plus it was a glorious morning for bird hunting.

"Can you get anyone else?"

No, was the reply.

A thought popped into my mind, but it violated a couple of cardinal rules. "Hold on for a second," I said. I worked through the possible downside to the plan that was starting to take shape. "Is the guy there?"

"Standing right here."

"Put him on."

I introduced myself and asked the guy where he was from. Chicago. Lots of fly fishermen from Chicago. I asked if he hunted. He didn't hunt. I told him that I had made plans and that I had a new bird dog, my first dog in nearly fifteen years, and that every hour of the season was precious. But I also told him that I planned to do a little fishing that day. So I explained the deal. I would spend the day with him, but only if I could get in some hunting. That was okay with him, he'd tag along. Always wanted to see a dog work. So far so good. Next question: Could he roll cast? Yes, but only so-so. Then I asked him if he had his heart set on fishing the river. Not really, he just wanted to get in some fishing on the last day of the season. It was only his second time in the area and he was willing to try anything. Perfect.

"I have one more question and you may think this one is a little weird."

"Try me," he said. Even over the phone I was beginning to like him. But you never know.

"Would you be willing to be blindfolded for part of the way?"

There was a pause, then, "Are you serious?"

Like a heart attack, I assured him.

He laughed and said, "Hell yes!"

To save time I had the guys at the fly shop fix him up with what he needed and agreed to meet him at a designated bridge. He got lost on the way to the bridge and was twenty minutes late. But he turned out to be a good guy; a young attorney-type just beginning to make some serious money. And like so many of his ilk these days, he had fallen for the mysteries of the long rod. But there was not a sniff of yuppie about him, and I sniffed pretty good.

I explained to him that he would simply have to take my word that we would have a good time, and at the end of the day he could pay me whatever he thought the day was worth. It turned out he liked dogs, but the highrise in which he lived (on Lakeshore Avenue) didn't permit pets. And he said he wouldn't have one anyway under the circumstances. He and goofball became instant friends.

It was a merry trio that loaded into the truck and headed for one of my favorite grouse coverts. I explained that I wanted to hunt first and close the day at what I hoped would be kind of a special place. He was thrilled just to be heading into the woods and obliged Casey Jones by scratching his face and ears every time the furry one stuck his head into the cab through the open beer window. Goofus was delighted to have some extra company. In fact, we had hunted alone since opening day when our pal Pete had the pleasure and honor of seeing him point (sort of) and retrieve (sort of) his first grouse.

"Why did you want to know if I could roll cast?" our pleasant sport asked.

"Have you ever fished a beaver pond?"

"No, but I've read about it."

I explained about the pond I had found and said that he was going to get a chance to fish it.

"That's where the blindfold comes in I take it?" He was smiling broadly.

I was actually having second thoughts about the blindfold. He'd gotten lost on the way to the bridge and I knew there was no way on God's green earth that this city kid was going to find his way back to my (how quickly we become possessive) beaver pond.

"We'll see," I replied.

It was one of those beautiful September mornings in the north woods, with the air sharp and crisp and the aspens ablaze with yellow. But best of all there were grouse and woodcock around and Casey Jones had a couple of near-perfect points and the little double also pointed where it was supposed to. Our new friend was tickled, even though the blaze orange stocking cap I had given him kept hanging up in the brush and coming off. "I don't know if I could get into this," he said once as he picked up the cap, "but it's really interesting watching the dog and, what the hell, it's a gorgeous day. I appreciate you bringing me along."

We broke for lunch and I wiped down the shotgun and put it away. I explained to the dog—as he was enjoying a small pile of biscuits—that he would have to stay in the truck for part of the afternoon. He acted like he didn't hear me.

It took the better part of an hour to reach the pond. I didn't blindfold our sport and I really think he would have volunteered for the rack rather than try to remember the way there. Dirt roads turned to two-trackers, and a final two-tracker turned into an old fire trail as we bumped along at snail speed. I was subtly eyeballing just days-old blaze marks, and if our guest saw them, he didn't say anything.

Finally I stopped and shut off the motor.

"I hope you don't have a heart attack on me because I could never find my way out of here," murmured our trout fisherman. Then he said, "I hear water. What is it?"

"The stuff of dreams," I said, and I wasn't trying to be dramatic. "Let's rig up."

There is something unbelievably haunting about re-mote beaver ponds, at least to me. They are invariably placid and beautiful and full of secrets. When the beavers make them they create a little world unto itself. To intrude upon a wilderness beaver pond is to insert yourself into this spe-cial place, and no human does it well. Lakes and streams have a way of hiding the ineptitude of the fisherman. Beaver ponds make you pay for every indiscretion, no matter how slight. The exception is the pond that—as far as a trout population is concerned—is in the last stage of its life. That's when the original stream bed has silted over, killing most of the indigenous aquatic insect life. Any trout still there are literally starving to death. Anything that lands in the water is usually a goner. (True, some ponds have long lives. Lucky you, if you have one. I had one once.)

We left Casey Jones in the truck. He was less disturbed than I thought he would be. We hiked down the hill and there it was and I heard a "Wow!" from behind me. It was a spontaneous, reverent wow and I felt even less like I'd made a mistake.

The surface of the pond was a patchwork of color: streaks of white, rippling nosegays of yellow, a splash of red, broad wipes of cadmium blue. And here and there punctuated by the small, quiet circles of rising trout.

I put our rusty roll caster in a small open spot in the shadows and told him not to chase rise forms; just put the fly out and let it sit. A little twitch every so often might help. I had put a 7X tippet on both of our leaders. I tied a #18 parachute Adams on his tippet and a #20 Elk Hair Caddis on mine.

I went up near the dam and actually found a spot where I had room to backcast. Mindful of the rises near the center of the pond, I searched for what the trout might be taking, but saw nothing.

The fly line snaked beautifully through the narrow opening in the woods behind me and, in fact, I marveled at the whiteness of it unfurling against the green background of a stand of young pines. I was giddy to be in this place and each act seemed to be magnified and took on a pleasure of its own. The fly dropped gently on the water, here and there, pulled more quickly toward the dam as my casts lengthened toward what was once the main channel.

Finally the fly disappeared in a gentle sip and I was fast to a trout. It flashed around the deeper water behind the dam and after a time came to the bank. I lifted it onto the grass. It was a brown of about ten inches, golden and shining next to a pinkish stalk of bouncing bet.

A moment later I heard a "whoop" and saw a trout thrashing on the surface up the pond. The wind carried a muffled "oh man!" as the trout was pulled onto shore.

I caught three more trout, all brookies, and was more than satisfied. At intervals I had walked up to see how the other pond fisherman was doing, helping once to unsnarl a leader and tie on a new tippet. His first trout had been a brookie; he managed to catch another and lost one.

Late afternoon we called it quits and walked up to the truck, stowed our gear, and let the pooch out. He stretched, lifted a leg on a tire, and headed for the pond just like he knew it was there. We followed for a last look and to my delight my new pond-fishing expert turned into a bartender, producing a pint of Jack Daniels from a kit bag.

We sat in the grass above the pond and passed the hooch back and forth. He also passed me a wad of bills. I tried to pass it back.

"No way," he said. "I would have paid twice that just to see this spot. I can't tell you what this has meant to me. I'll never forget it. The day, I mean." We both laughed.

We watched the big, handsome lad, Casey Jones, circle the pond, moving through the birch and aspen like a ghost, and I wondered if I was dreaming.

❖

A month after the opening day of trout season the following spring, on a rare day off, I retraced my way through the maze of two-trackers, pretty much remembering the way, but guided still by faded blaze marks.

The scent of Casey Jones was still in the truck. His hairs had worked into the upholstery, and despite numerous cleanings I would smell him every time I opened the door, especially now that it was getting warm. I had a bottle of Jack Daniels on the seat next to me. There were still patches of snow in the woods, but the trail was open.

The truck chugged slowly along and I chugged a toast to Pat Dwyer, the good friend and veterinarian who had determined that it had been either a brain tumor or epilepsy. It had started with little fits and then progressed to big, prolonged attacks, and it broke my heart to see a dog suffer like that. Finally he was on so much phenobarbital that he was only the Casey Jones I once knew for moments a day, as one dose wore off and it was near time for another. We reveled together during those rare moments. Then finally nothing worked, and one day he had an attack that didn't end until he lay quivering from exhaustion. I held him until he was quiet and then drove the big guy, only sixteen months old, to the local vet, unable to postpone the inevitable any longer. Pat, two hundred miles away, had suffered through weekly visits and daily phone calls with me.

I reached the clearing and with hooch in hand started down the hill, remembering how C. J. had bailed out of the truck to point a flock of turkeys, and wondering now about that sort of determination and what it might have meant had he lived.

It occurred to me then that something was wrong, and I knew instantly what it was. I could not hear the water running through the dam. Moments later I saw why. The pond had been abandoned and the dam had all but washed out in the spring thaw. The beavers had felled and used most of the aspen near the pond and had moved on. A depressing basin of black muck with the little creek flowing dirty through the center of it was all that remained.

The sensible part of me chucked the whole thing off. That's Mother Nature. The beavers ran out of food and looked for more grub elsewhere. But I was depressed beyond words. Following that tragic visit to the vet a few months earlier the pond had become a symbol to me. The symbol of a time, however brief, that stood for the way things should be but, indeed, rarely are. Remembering moments of near-mystic perfection during that short time added to the gloom.

I followed the creek aimlessly upstream, more to get away from that disheartening black muck than anything else, and finally came to it in its natural setting, here only a foot deep. Mr. Daniels and I followed along, and after half an hour or so the meadow opened into a wonderful, almost alpinelike setting.

The creek was a mere three or four feet wide with lots of bends and undercut banks, and my spirits rose slightly. This would be fun with a nice long rod that would let you stay back from the bank and probe those dark little undercuts with maybe a small Hare's Ear Nymph below a tiny split-shot.

And then I heard it. That distinctive gurgle that can only mean one thing. And then the dam came into sight, a big one because the meadow was wide here. Fresh aspen were down everywhere. The dam was nearly as high as my head on the downstream side. Water seeped through the dam in a number of places creating an intriguing delta of sparkling ministreams at its base. I found a log in the cold, spring sunlight and Mr. Daniels and I reposed for a time. Then trout began to rise, six or eight out over the original creek channel. I stood, fished the dog collar out of the coat pocket, and threw it as far as I could into the center of the pond. I sipped the last of the J. D., remembered C. J., and felt better.

8

❖

THE GHOST OF
HENRY FORD

The North Branch of Michigan's Au Sable River is generally known as the more "gentle" of the three major branches. Yet I've had more adventure along its banks than nearly anywhere else.

I think it has something to do with the ghost of Henry Ford. Some people *might* claim that the old auto baron's ghost would be expected to hang out at the Henry Ford Museum near Detroit. Maybe. But I put the ghost of Henry Ford a few hundred miles north, on the North Branch of the Au Sable River. At least during trout fishing season.

At some point in his life Henry Ford owned a lodge or belonged to a club on the North Branch. There are references connecting him to "The Au Sable Trout and Game Club." It was on the east bank of the river at a place called Dam Four. That's still the name of the place and the remains of the old dam are still there. I'm guessing that the dam is a leftover from Michigan's post-Civil War logging era. Many of these old "lowhead" dams were built to raise the water in a particular stretch of river. This helped float the logs on their way downstream to a mill or railhead.

There exists a photo of Henry Ford which I presume was taken at the club. He is standing on some sort of streamside platform in high lace boots and sporting the outdoor livery of the time. There isn't a trace of a tree in the background, just the knee-high slash so characteristic of Michigan's landscape following the lumbering days. Henry the First appears to be in his early- to mid-thirties. He is sort of grinning, as though he might be having a good time.

He is known to have liked the outdoors and in his later years, following his huge success, he went on annual camping trips with Thomas Edison, Harvey Firestone, and John Burroughs. That is, if you could call them camping trips. It was pretty luxurious camping, complete with electric lights. Imagine, vehicles by Ford, tires by Firestone, electric generators by Edison, and natural history by Burroughs.

I had been fascinated by the man since I first read a biography about him in junior high school. Here was basically a farm boy who created, from scratch, one of America's corporate giants. Over the years I read more about him. We cheer the Bill Gateses of today for their successes, but where is the drama, the passion? Where are the tough, hard men who forged an industry from iron and steel and changed a nation forever? Where would we find men today who would fight the Battle of the Overpass?

The remains of the old lodge stood there on the bank for many years. What was once a private road leading into the club has been a public access for decades, so it was possible to park right at the structure. It was a large, two-story frame building. That it was a frame building is interesting. You would think that back then log structures would have been the rule. But there was a time in some parts of northern Michigan when you couldn't find a log. The forest had been leveled.

A porch ran along the entire front barely a yard from the bank. Whoever sat there on that porch in those bygone days could look nearly straight down at the river. Inside, on the first floor, were several large rooms. In my mind's eye

I could see Henry Ford sitting in a corner with his cronies, talking about things that would impact the world. Upstairs there were bedrooms and I tried to imagine where he slept. Finally, the place was so tumbledown it was too dangerous to even go up those stairs.

I fished there often, especially at hopper time. It's mostly meadow water downstream, very pretty and easy wading.

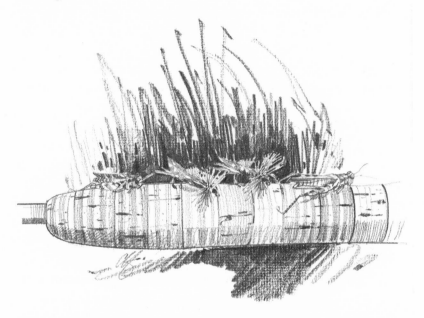

My amigo, the late Craig Woods, loved this stretch of the Au Sable. He'd come out from Vermont and, invariably, suggest that we go fish at Mr. Ford's place, where once, as he recorded in his little book, *The River as Looking Glass & Other Stories From the Outdoors,* we caught "unspeakable numbers of trout." We had stumbled into a hatch of little Blue-winged Olives that came off for the entire afternoon and the trout never stopped feeding.

There wasn't a monster among them but we didn't care. Woody did take a nice fish in a little logjam on the side of an island going downstream. It was a minipool against the bank on an S curve with a log that straddled the channel just above the surface. Naturally, the two trout that were rising were below the log. It was a very difficult place to put a fly. But Woody did it and one of the trout smacked the fly just as it popped over the log. I can't even guess how many trout we caught between the two of us that day. "Unspeakable numbers," as Woody wrote. We walked back to the car along the bank at dusk and soon passed the old lodge.

"I can feel his presence," Woody said quietly.

"I do, every time," I replied.

Woody and I fished together many times, both in Michigan and Vermont. He was a remarkable editor and writer, a gifted, learned person and—more importantly—a good friend. He left us too soon.

❖

It was also here that Paul Lienert and I were chased by a goon I'll call Ralph.

One sunny summer Saturday Paul and I were trying to figure out where we could go to escape an obnoxious canoe hatch on the main stream of the Au Sable.

"Hell, let's go up to the North Branch," I suggested.

So naturally we ended up at Dam Four, and as we parked the car, I noticed some changes at the access.

First, wire had been strung alongside the access right down to the river. There were also "No Trespassing" signs everywhere. And there was a good old boy sitting in a pickup truck who obviously wasn't there to fish—as we were about to find out.

Paul and I rigged up. I wanted to walk upstream a mile or so through the woods and fish back down. There were paths along both banks and no cabins or homes on either bank for some distance. The river twists through hardwoods up there, shallow and clear, over fine gravel. It's not big-fish material, but it's classic, beautiful, dry-fly water with a hint of the wild about it.

I started toward the path. Paul said, "Are you sure this is okay?"

I assured him that I'd been walking up this bank for nearly twenty years.

Before we even got to the wire I heard a door slam and someone yell "Hey you!" It was our sport from the pickup truck, hotfooting it our way.

"That's private property there! You can't go that way!"

"What are you talking about," I said. "I've been fishing here for twenty years."

"You can fish, but you gotta get in the river over there." He was pointing at the short flight of steps that led from the parking area down to the river.

"But I'm going up a mile or so."

"It don't matter! You got to stay off the bank!"

"Then I'll walk up the other bank."

"That's private too! Try it and I'll call the sheriff!"

My mind was working overtime and I'd already reached the conclusion that I wasn't going to be run out of a place that I'd been fishing for damn near twenty years.

"What's your name?" I asked our enthusiastic sentry.

"Ralph," he said.

"Ralph," I said, "are you trying to tell me that I'm supposed to wade a mile upstream?"

"That's up to you."

"Who the hell do you work for?"

Ralph hesitated for a moment. "Mr. Adams." (We'll call him that.)

I explained to Ralph that both he and his boss probably knew that I could get out of the river anytime I wanted to in order to get around holes I couldn't wade. I'm no expert on riparian law, but I knew that much. Lienert, an auto writer, was taking all this in. Naturally, we had a test-drive vehicle with us. It was a shiny new number, a great vehicle for getting trout fishermen comfortably to and from trout streams. I wondered if getting pinched by Ralph would be the lead in his next column.

It turned out that Ralph knew his riparian rights, too.

"That's right, you can get out and go around, but then you gotta get right back in," he said.

I could see he was getting steamed.

I said, "You know that we can't possibly wade through there." I pointed at the deep hole by the old dam. "We'll just walk up the path aways."

Ralph was turning red.

I ducked under the wire and started down the trail with Paul right behind me. Somewhere, inside me, some ancient Viking genes were stirring. For indeed there was something medieval about these shenanigans. The wealthy duke was trying to keep the serfs from the sacred water. No matter that the serfs had been walking these banks for more than a hundred years. No matter that the woods were big enough there so that a small army of serfs could tramp around and not bother a soul. No matter that the duke's castle wasn't even near that stretch of the river and he couldn't possibly be bothered by two serfs he would never see. No matter that the serfs in question were two genteel fly fishermen and not a pack of Hell's Angels or, even worse, commercial canoeists. It was abundantly clear that the duke wanted his very own private trout stream.

Ralph was hot on our heels and the moment we came to shallow water he started screaming "Get off the bank! Get off the bank or I'll call the sheriff!"

I suggested to Paul that we wade up a couple of bends and let Ralph cool down. Then we'd hop right up on the opposite bank and continue on our way.

We trudged along against the current. I was beginning to get hot, in more ways than one. Shallow or not, the river zips right along there and wading was work. I looked around but I couldn't see Ralph, so up on the bank we went.

We took about three deliciously easy steps on that well-worn little path when, from the woods across the stream, came "Get off the damn bank or I'm going to call the sheriff! Right now!"

"Go ahead, call the sheriff, Ralph!" I hollered back.

"Do you think he'll do it?" asked Paul.

"Who cares!" I said. But we got back in the river and waded up another few bends. Then I'd really had enough. I got back up on the bank. Paul was close behind me.

"If he does call the sheriff, what's the sheriff going to do?" I said. "If he wants to walk a mile through the woods what's he going to find? Two nice guys fly fishing, standing in the middle of the river."

I thought it would be interesting, actually, to be sitting on the bank when the sheriff arrived. Our feet would be in the river, but our asses would be on the duke's land. How would the law sort that out? I had another bone to pick as well: The duke's bailiff was parked and operating from the serf's turf, that is, a public access. I wondered how the duke would explain how his bailiff could harass and threaten people who were standing on the very ground their license fees had paid for? Yes, I was a real unhappy serf right about then.

We walked along the path for several peaceful moments, but I could hear Ralph skulking along the opposite bank. And then, lo and behold, just downstream, here comes Ralph running full-tilt across the river, splashing great geysers of water, scaring the hell out of any trout in the neighborhood. Trout with which Paul and I soon hoped to do some business. So much for that. Ralph jumped up on the bank and came running up the path. Paul and I jumped into the river.

Ralph was clearly upset. In fact, he was screaming. Plus, he was wet from the knees down, his shoes sloshing water.

He threatened us with everything from the FBI to the CIA to going up to the house to get his boss. I must say he was enthusiastic. The duke was getting his money's worth. I lit a cigar and suggested he go get the bossman. He went running off through the woods, dripping water. A tree had fallen into the river there, so I sat on the trunk and tied on a fly and lit a cigar. Paul, quite sensibly, started to fish.

About fifteen minutes later, there on the bank, appeared Ralph and the boss. The duke was smoking a big, fat cigar. His bailiff had a big, fat smirk.

The duke was a bit imperious, but not unfriendly, which clearly bothered his bailiff. (I think Ralph was hoping the boss would pull out a .357 and plug the two criminals right on the spot.)

I set my rod on the old blowdown, stepped up on the bank, stuck out my hand, and introduced myself to the duke, whereupon the duke and I discovered we had some mutual acquaintances.

I explained to the duke that I'd been a visitor to this stretch of the river for two decades, respected the stream and the land, came and went quietly, leaving both the river and the forest the same way I found it.

The duke nodded. His bailiff turned crimson. Smoke came out of his ears. Precedent aside, I suggested to the duke that he owed me one anyway. His eyebrows raised. "How so!?"

It was simple. Two of the duke's vassals had once gotten out of the river at my family's place on the main branch and, walking up the lawn, said they were friends of the duke and were told that they could get out there. Back then, I'd never heard of the duke, but apparently his knaves thought that they could exit the river anywhere if they dropped the duke's name. We are a convenient four-hour wade downstream from an access, at the end of the road that leads directly back to the landing. We usually give permission to fishermen who ask if they can get out of the river there. Good manners help, but the duke's vassals were already halfway to the road. What would have been the point in saying no?

The duke was surprised. (The duke's bailiff was coming unglued. Because of his efforts, nothing short of a lynching was going to satisfy him.) In the end, the serf and the duke struck a deal. The serf could walk the duke's banks. For the record, the serf would have done it anyway, for many reasons, despite the unpleasant bailiff and the threat of visiting sheriffs.

❖

I guess the problem with trouble is that it finds you when you least expect it. For the most part, we all avoid the obvious. We get out of the stream and walk around holes that appear too deep for safe wading. We don't try to pet large, wild animals. We don't walk around barefoot near our fly-tying desks. Those sorts of things.

But there I was, on another occasion, walking along the bank of the gentle North Branch of Michigan's Au Sable River, filling a pipe with tobacco. The pipe was one of those curved stem models that hang so easily from your mouth, a favorite of mine for fishing.

It was early in the season and I had stopped the car on the bridge at the little crossroads village of Lovells to check the river. Voila! Trout were rising upstream and down, but especially up. There were a couple of promising fish working just at the base of the old low-head logging dam. The usual pint-size brook trout were also there, splashily rising and even flinging themselves through the air. The lessons of the kingfisher and the great blue heron had yet to be learned.

I had actually been on my way up to a section of the stream called the Sheep Ranch, but a trout that is rising is worth two that may not be, as they say, so I hastily parked the car and rigged up. It was chilly and a rainy drizzle fell intermittently. I wasn't sure what was hatching, but

I scrambled down the bank next to the bridge and started upstream. There was a well-worn trail along the bank. I reached the old dam (more like a low spillway) and saw even more—and I thought better—trout working above it. So I hurried along, packing a bowl of tobacco as I went. I had a serious case of ESI (Early Season Itch).

Suddenly the earth gave way beneath me. I went straight down, right up to my armpits. The pipe, tobacco pouch, and rod went flying. The rod—fortunately as it turned out—was within reach. For a moment there I freaked out. Long-forgotten movie scenes from my childhood involving death by quicksand flashed in my mind.

Instinctively, I'd thrown my arms out and soon realized I wasn't sinking any deeper. In fact, my feet seemed to be on something reasonably solid. But I was stuck, the lower two-thirds of me immobile.

In Michigan, along the edges of some trout streams, you sometimes find a rich, black muck. The Lord of The Mayflies, Mr. Hexagenia limbata, loves it. But you want to avoid stepping in it. Usually you sink ankle-deep or part-way to your knees. It's tough enough getting out of the stuff even then. I'd heard rumors about places like the one I had just—unfortunately—discovered, but those had been rumors. Until now. So that's what I got for not watching where I was going while packing a pipe.

It's funny what you think of once you realize you're not going to suffocate in a pit of ooze, not that I actually thought for more than a few moments that I might. (It was just those first few microseconds and that long-ago image of those writhing hands disappearing in the quicksand.) No, my worst fear was that some fisherman-friend would come along with an Instamatic in his vest. And he, of course, would insist on taking my picture prior to helping me out of the hole.

I wriggled and wiggled to no avail. The hole was just wide enough that I couldn't get my arms on anything solid.

A good twenty minutes elapsed and I was still solidly stuck. I can't say that I was beginning to panic again, but I was seriously starting to wonder just how in the hell I was going to get unstuck.

There was a sapling about six feet away and I thought if I could somehow reach it, I might be able to lever myself free.

It took a lot of willpower to stick one arm down into that goo and get my streamer box. I clipped back my leader, tied on the biggest streamer I could find, and left it hanging a few inches from the tip of the fly rod. I reached out with the rod and hooked the sapling near the top. Slowly, I began to pull it toward me, going hand-over-hand up the fly rod. It made me sick to do it, but I had to let the fly rod sink into the muck.

The sapling bent, bent some more, kept coming, and when it was close enough, I reached up and grabbed it. I pulled the rod out of the muck and set it aside and got two hands firmly on that little tree. It had small, bright green leaves that were just beginning to unfurl. I could smell the leaves. They smelled clean and fresh.

I struggled and finally began to inch my way out of the goo. Actually, I was coming out of my waders. That muck had so much suction that it kept the waders trapped. The sapling broke, but it was green and held together. Inch by inch I wriggled out. I got a knee up on something solid, and with a good push, popped free.

I stood, took a deep breath, and looked around. I hadn't strayed from the path by more than a few feet. I wondered how many other hapless fishermen might have stumbled into that pit?

With some difficulty I pulled the waders out of that sucking ooze and walked in my stocking feet to the river, being very careful where I stepped. I tried to rinse everything off, but the battle damage had been great. There haven't been too many times I've walked away from rising trout, but this repair work had to be done in dry dock.

❖

I always thought that somewhere along the line I'd learn more about old Henry the First and his fly fishing days on the North Branch, time stolen from his sprawling empire. But then one day, in an obscure little book, I inadvertently discovered a reference to his fishing. The author, who knew him firsthand, wrote that Mr. Ford liked to fish, but if he "didn't catch something in the first five minutes" he'd give up. He was an "impatient" fisherman. That didn't sound like a fly fisherman to me. Frankly, I didn't want to know more.

The lodge is long gone. There's still a cement casement at the foot of the bank that housed a waterwheel for generating electricity. It was said to have been designed by Henry Ford's friend Thomas Edison.

Sometimes, when the crumbling old place was still there, I'd come up the river from below and half expect to see the titan puttering about in the twilight or taking his ease on the porch.

I like to think of him as a fly fisherman. On those evenings when I paused at the front entrance to the tattered old structure, the door off its hinges, I could have sworn his spirit was about.

One evening I took a big brown below the islands in the deep pool on the west bank. The fish took the fly— a hopper—tight against the bank. It ran out of the pool and on below. There was a trick to wading around that bend. There was exactly one spot you could go through without going in over your waders. I found it, got around the bend, and finally into the shallower water below. Five or ten minutes later I had it, a thick brown trout of perhaps eighteen inches. It was my best fish ever on the North Branch and it was the first trout I'd ever taken out of that pool.

An hour later, walking back to the car, I came up to the lodge. Passing the entrance I heard a noise and looked in. There, in the dark, was the silhouette of a man peering through a rear window at the silent meadow. I stood glued to the spot. Finally, the figure turned, came toward me, then suddenly stopped. "Hey!" said the figure. I jumped.

"Hello," I said.

"You gave me a start."

"Likewise."

The figure turned into a fly fisherman as he came out on the porch. He had a beer in one hand and a sandwich in the other. He raised his beer and sort of saluted the old place. "Must have been something in its day," he said.

9

A Hex On You

Fly fishing at night is not a natural thing to do, although a case might be made that any kind of fishing at night is anomalous. Nevertheless, over the course of two decades, I have done my share of stumbling around in the dark: getting lost, falling in, breaking tackle, getting eaten alive by mosquitoes and black flies, tangling with bats (two), nearly catching myself and a forest on fire, getting chased by a raccoon (which I would have sworn was a bear), but most often, simply standing waist deep in trout water doing absolutely nothing. Hour after hour of standing silently in the dark and doing nothing—not even *fishing* let alone *catching*. Once I took a nonfishing girlfriend with me (she insisted), and about an hour after midnight she, quite rightly, declared that I was "a f——— lunatic," doing the "stupidest f——— thing" she'd ever seen in her life. Up to that moment, the most colorful thing I'd ever heard her say was "darn it!"

She stood there next to me in oversized waders, water up to her ample chest, swigging Beaujolais straight from one of the bottles we were supposed to be saving for later.

I patiently tried to explain that you had to see what happens when…

"Don't even try. Give me the car keys. I'm getting the hell out of here," she commanded.

In his book *Aquatic Entomology: The Fishermen's and Ecologists' Illustrated Guide to Insects and Their Relatives,* Patrick McCafferty tells us that the cause of all this late-night nonsense, the giant mayfly, *Hexagenia limbata,* is a "common burrower." And in what might be the most understated sentence in the entire literature of aquatic insects, he writes, "They *may* leave their burrows at night." (Emphasis mine.) *May.* Now there's the key word if there ever was one. Our man McCafferty appears to be referring to the feeding habits of the nymph. However, I'm more concerned about the sex life of this bug, particularly as it relates to me leaving *my* burrow at night. It seems that the same declaration applies. As any addict of this hatch can tell you, when it comes to frolic, Mr. and Mrs. Hexagenia limbata can be extraordinarily capricious. They most often seem to leave their little hidy-holes the night you're not there. Or, if they do decide to do their thing, they will most likely do it where you aren't.

Well, the good Mr. McCafferty can tell us that the mayfly *Hexagenia limbata* is a "common burrower," but the behavior it causes among fly fishermen is anything but common.

At the beginning of each season I say to myself, the hell with it, I'm not fishing the Hex hatch this year. Then, of course, I remember that five-pounder from three years ago. Or that three-pounder two years ago. Or that six-pounder last year.

❖

In northern Michigan, the annual hatch of this giant mayfly is responsible for a sort of low-key, summer version of deer season. But instead of stumbling around in the woods by day, the participants stumble around in the water at night, because this bug is mostly nocturnal. The big mayfly is found in the waters of many states. But I do not know if it causes the same fuss elsewhere.

Around the middle of June in Michigan's trout country, motels begin to fill, campgrounds start to swell. The whole north country is astir, on edge with anticipation.

Everywhere, you hear conversations like "Someone said they came off just below town last night" or "I saw a few of them on the streetlight outside the bar" or "A guy at the restaurant said that his buddy said that they came off the upper South Branch three nights ago" and most often "Should be any time now."

You find yourself getting caught up in this special form of madness. You can't help it. Because when the Hex hatches, it triggers a trout feeding-frenzy, an absolute orgy of trout gluttony. Best of all, it brings out the truly large fish, the monsters that you rarely see during normal summer office hours.

It also brings out a rare form of fly fisherman, a person willing to sleep most of the day and fish a good part of the night. Someone willing to stake out one hole on a river, sometimes in the middle of the afternoon, to prevent anyone else from getting it. This someone has to be willing to stand for hours in basically one spot, hoping that sometime during the night the big bug will make an appearance.

Rarer forms of fly fishermen are those who fish only this hatch, who get the fly rods out but once a year. These are guys who wouldn't know a Quill Gordon from a March Brown. You see them mostly in the campgrounds along the river. They're often with their families—it's an annual outing. They've come up from Detroit or Grand Rapids or Toledo to fish the "caddis hatch." That's what they call it, especially the old-timers. (I've also heard the fly called by several other names: Sandfly, Michigan Spinner, Fishfly, and Giant Michigan Mayfly. As a kid growing up on Lake Erie, we called them Canadian Soldiers. The big lake had a tremendous hatch of them. We thought they came across the lake from Canada, a pesky gift from those mysterious Canadians. When they arrived they covered everything. My mother swept them from the screen doors and from the stoop. Roads along the lake would be slick with them, actually causing a hazard. Each summer during the sixties there were less of them, and finally one summer they came no more. Lake Erie had died, but we didn't know it.)

These once-a-year "caddis" fishermen have their favorite holes and logjams—having fished them for years—and often use their kids to stake them out. Sometime in the early afternoon, Pop will send son Johnnie in waders, with fly rod, to The Spot. Johnnie might actually throw a fly if there are any suspicious-looking fishermen nearby, just to legitimize his being there. Otherwise, he'll probably sit on the bank and listen to his boom box and drink Coke and eat candy bars. But quick as an otter, he'll be in the river in Pop's spot if someone comes along.

Sometime later he might be relieved by his brother Tommy, who pulls on the waders, takes the rod, and assumes the late-afternoon-to-early-evening watch.

It does occasionally happen that some son of a bitch will come along and try to run the kid out of the pool. "Hey kid, whatcha doin' in my hole? Vamoose!" Tommy might hold his ground, or more accurately, his water, but usually ends up running for Pop. There is then the possibility of all hell breaking loose. I once saw two guys duking it out midstream. Sometimes these things rekindle back in the campground and feuds develop. Mind you, these are odd occurrences, but if you hang out in any of the bars such as Spike's, Ma Deeter's, or Jack's Place during Hex time you'll hear scores of stories.

Barring that kind of calamity, Pop arrives just before dusk and finds that Tommy has successfully patrolled The Pool. Pop slips into the river and, as darkness descends, gets ready for the drama he hopes will soon unfold. Having slept most of the day, he's raring to go.

I was a participant in that scene for many years. It was a ritual that was observed each summer, an even bigger deal in some ways than opening day. But I eventually tired of finding a fisherman in every good pool. The good pools are finite. The Hex nymph lives in silt, sand, or mud. You won't find them in gravel. So that automatically places limitations on where you want to be. And many a snoopy fly fisherman before me discovered the good pools. Sure, I found some great spots and had some great times. But it got to the point where, no matter how remote the place, I began finding cars in the woods where I used to find none. That, of course, is the problem with having a home river that's famous. So I began to do the obvious. I began to explore elsewhere. A friend tipped me off to a sandy little creek in a cedar swamp that held some good fish. I discovered that it had one hell of a hatch of the big bugs. (Which he claimed he didn't know about. He never fished it at night.) Mr. and Mrs. Hex were as unpredictable there as anywhere, but that's part of the game and I didn't care. I had the place to myself and could roam from one pool to the next. One night I caught a brook trout that was a couple of honest inches past the twelve-inch marker on my rod, big for a Michigan brookie.

I kept exploring and found a few more hot spots. But the second-best place in my inventory I came across entirely by accident.

I was parked one day at a little creek that ran through a culvert under a dirt road, a half-hour from the house.

There was a good pool on either side of the road and I often stopped to fling a fly for a few minutes. I had never explored the creek, either up or down. I came across it one day as I was searching for a shortcut between home and work.

I'd given each pool five minutes (with no results) and was putting the fly rod back in the truck when along came a guy on a three-wheeler. He stopped and shut off his engine and turned out to be a chatty, retired fellow out for a ride in the sunshine. He had a bunch of wildflowers in the basket of his machine; his excuse, as it turned out, to go for a ride.

I hasten to add here, that I would shoot these RV-type machines on sight if I thought I could get away with it. I once considered having bumper stickers made that would say *Do The Earth A Favor—Run Over An RV Today*. But if an old man finds harmless pleasure in running around on dirt roads, picking wildflowers, that's okay with me. Especially in light of what happened.

He asked me if I'd had any luck. I said no.

"Have you ever fished the river upstream?"

My antennae began to vibrate. "No," I said again. "Do you know anything about it?"

"Not personally," he said. "I don't fish, but I've got a cabin just up the road and my neighbor is nuts for fishing. He comes here at night when that fishfly hatches. Brings home some big trout."

Bingo!

"Does he wade up from here?" I asked.

He pointed up the road. "There's a two-tracker right around the bend that follows the creek north. It's a lot wider up there."

We chatted for a bit and finally the old gent fired up the noisy monster and took off. I fired up the truck and a moment later turned onto the two-tracker. I spent the next two hours checking out the creek. There were some gravel stretches, but there was lots of sand and muck. It looked like Hex heaven.

I was back a month later, just at dusk on a Saturday night.

There wasn't a soul around as I parked the truck in a small clearing, not ten yards from the stream. It was unnerving to have the place to myself.

The rod was already rigged, so all I had to do was pull on the hip boots, slip on the vest, check the cigar pocket, and put on some bug dope. I always apply bug dope with the *back* of my hands. There isn't any place on your face, neck, or arms that you can't reach with the back of one hand or the other. It's actually very easy, and it keeps your palms and fingers free of the vile stuff, and so keeps it off flies, leaders, and fly lines.

In the stream, which was about twenty feet wide there, I checked the point on the hook and greased the fly again. I'd done that once already at home. The pattern was tied on a #2 long-shank streamer hook. I also had patterns in sizes four and six. I prefer the style of Hex pattern that has deer hair running parallel with the hook, with the tying thread crisscrossed around the body. I like a little clump of hair coming off the end of the shank, which helps float that heavy hook. The tails are long, about an inch and a half. Give me some hackle up front and a couple of large grizzly wings, or even better, a pretty, upright, parachute-style wing of white deer hair. I'm not sure that it makes a bit of difference to the trout, but I know that I feel better if the belly of the fly is yellow.

Some fishermen like clipped deer hair bodies, and I've seen flies that had dubbing for the body. But I've never seen a clipped body that has the sleek silhouette of the natural. I've tied and used flies with dubbed bodies, but in my opinion it's too difficult to keep them floating.

It got dark and I stood and waited. I was near the end of a relatively straight stretch of the stream, just above a big, dark pool full of logs and brush that had obviously been collecting there for years. The creek made a sharp left and then a right. That pile of debris wedged in the turn was an excellent trout hotel, but a potential nightmare if a hooked fish got back under all that stuff. My leader was a six-foot piece of eight-pound mono. I wouldn't hesitate to put the skids to a good fish if I got lucky and it came to that.

Everyone has their own way of doing things, but when it comes to the Hex hatch I don't like to fish until something happens, or I'm ready to leave if nothing does. Some fishermen will start throwing the fly the minute it gets dark. I don't, because I don't want junior-size trout tearing up the fly and tearing around in the water. The only reason I'm there is for a shot at the big fish that this hatch can produce. You can always smoke cigars and think about sex. Or, if you're so inclined, you might take an occasional nip from the medicinal flask, just to help keep the hobgoblins away.

I must tell you that, as I stood there in the dark, I had grave doubts, and I'm as optimistic a fisherman as you'll ever meet. I'd happily fish in a mud puddle and expect to catch something. But I had driven up the two-tracker some distance before I doubled back to the place I eventually parked. I wanted to see if there were any other fishermen around. Had there been any cars parked near the stream, I'd have made a mental note and returned some other day for a look-see. Not that I was planning on stealing anyone's hole, but there's usually a reason people fish where they do. During the Hex hatch it often has something to do with big fish. But there wasn't another vehicle anywhere. And the hatch had been on for over a week on waters elsewhere. Even though I was back in the boondocks to an extent, the turn-off onto the two-tracker was only *minutes* from a major highway, and not that much farther from one of my favorite watering holes.

I wondered if my informant had his creeks correct. I knew from looking at my county map that my waterway was a feeder creek that came out of a small lake with a certain fishy name and flowed into the north branch of the Eyeforget River. (The main branch being somewhat famous, but less so than its more illustrious cousin, as we all know.)

Or was it possible I had "discovered" a "secret" spot? I already had one of those, a little creek tucked away in a small valley, as far out in the middle of nowhere as it's possible to get these days. I'm not sure a fisherman should be allowed to have more than one such place.

I've said it before, and I'll say it again: There's no sound quite like a large trout feeding on the surface at night. The word "sip" is used quite often to describe trout taking mayflies on a summer afternoon, gentle rings appearing here and there. Trout do not sip when it comes time to dine on Mr. Hex. "Attack" would be a far better word.

Somewhere up behind me a good fish fed. And suddenly the air was full of bugs.

It always shocks me how big these mayflies are. When they're close you can actually hear them flapping their wings. They were everywhere, swarming over the stream, riding the current into the pool below. Two or three trout immediately began feeding there. More trout fed upstream. It was shallow up there, but even large trout will move into thin water at night in pursuit of these bugs.

I waited and listened. I already had line out, the exact amount that would let my pattern float just to the edge of the pool below. The fly tugged in the hook keeper.

Trout were feeding everywhere. I couldn't tell how many were feeding in the logjam, but several for sure. They all sounded like good fish.

I let my first cast go straight downstream, checking it just before the fly landed to give it a few feet of drag-free float. The fly line straightened, then bellied around and I knew the fly had floated past the jam.

I picked it up and cast again. Still nothing. I cast several more times with no luck. I knew what was happening. My fly was competing with a horde of naturals that were being carried into that pool. There were probably hundreds of struggling flies swirling around in that eddy.

On perhaps my tenth cast I had a vicious little strike that turned out to be an honest twelve-inch brown, a fish I'd normally celebrate on lighter tackle in the sunshine.

But tonight it fell into the dink category. I caught its slightly larger cousin a few moments later.

I lengthened the cast by a couple of feet and threw a little to the left. I couldn't see the fly land, but there was a big splash and the fly line tightened. I set the hook and all hell broke loose. The rod whipped into a shaking curve as the trout fishtailed near the logs. Instead of going for the jam, it bolted downstream, around the bend. I followed, trying to keep the fish on a short line. It was pitch black and I wasn't sure what was around the corner, but around we went. The reel squealed as the trout tore off line.

Around the bend the stream opened up even more and was very shallow. The trout got over to the right bank, where there appeared to be slightly deeper water, and bulldogged. It held there for a minute or two and then made another, short, run. And then it just seemed to quit. This has happened to me once or twice before with big trout and makes me wonder if trout age like people, assuming size has something to do with longevity. Do they lose their strength as they age? A question for my friend John Norcross, biologist/curmudgeon of the Au Sable River, who would probably have something to say about trout geriatrics.

I pumped the fish over the gravel until it lay at my feet. I wanted to see it, of course, and turned on the flashlight. It flopped around between my feet, a wonderfully spotted brown trout as long as my forearm, fat as a football. The tape read $19\frac{1}{4}$ inches.

The fly was firmly embedded in the corner of its jaw, one of the wings missing. I removed it and, holding the fish upright, faced it into the current. Several minutes later it swam slowly into the darkness.

I tied on a new fly, shut off the flashlight, and waited for my night vision to return. I walked upstream, and to avoid wading past the logjam, cut across what I thought was solid ground on the east bank. It turned out to be black, oozy muck. My foot caught on something and down I went, in a sprawl, burying my rod, and part of myself, in the goo.

I got to my feet, found the stream, and rinsed my tackle and as much of myself as I could. I then took just a nip of that snakebite medicine and fired up a cigar, destroying my night vision once again.

About fifteen minutes later, back in position, I shot a cast upstream where several fish were feeding steadily. I had an explosive strike the moment the fly landed, and was fast to some demon that bolted around the stream. This fish really fought. It jumped a couple of times and ripped out a fair amount of line. I forgot, momentarily, about being muddy and wet. The trout kept racing upstream, as though it was determined to find some spot to hole up. I moved slowly with it, but pumping every time it stopped. I gained ground and the current helped.

It came down and bolted past me, the leader straining on the short line. I lowered the tip to ease some of the strain on the leader. Finally I got it, fighting still, into shallow water. Running my fingers down the leader, I found the fly and got my other hand around the trout. It was nearly a twin of the other slob, but not as plump. This brown was sleek and hard and had a mean-looking hooked jaw. It taped out at nineteen inches even.

I continued to fish and took several more trout, including a brookie that topped the twelve-inch marker on my rod by about an inch.

The hatch tapered off, although I could hear fish working downstream. Wet and muddy, I trudged across the creek to my truck and grabbed a branch on the bank to pull myself up. The branch, which had been dead for at least fifty years, broke instantly, and down I went again.

Driving out, wet nearly to my knees, I debated about stopping at that conveniently located tavern mentioned earlier. My wet clothes would surely attract attention. But what the hell, I was thirsty. So I began concocting lies.

Okay, you say—that was your second-best spot. What about your first-best spot?

To be honest with you, I can't bring myself to write about it. Don't boo. I'm not doing this to tease you. It's just that this spot is extraordinarily unique. I would deliberately have to be so sketchy that you'd have a skeleton of a story, a tale with no flesh and blood. My compadre of many a bizarre adventure, the infamous Doc Elliott, ex-Yellowstone guide and this planet's true trout bum, showed me this honeyhole. I owe him a big one—forever. But I kid you not when I tell you that six- and eight-pound browns are considered undersize. Honest. You ought to hear what a ten-pound brown trout sounds like, feeding on the surface at night.

I continue, every season, to bumble around in the dark, catching my share, getting skunked more often than not, chasing this mysterious, big mayfly. It's a sickness. If you're not one of the afflicted, I say a Hex on you.

10

❖

Song of the
South Branch

Every Michigander knows that the lower half of his state is shaped like the back of a left-handed mitten. If you were to draw a line from the tip of the thumb on Lake Huron, straight west to the city of Ludington on Lake Michigan, you'd more or less divide the Lower Peninsula in half. You get the bottom half; I get the top half. Now take the index finger of your right hand and put it at the exact center of my part. If you missed the town of Grayling by more than half an inch I'll buy you lunch. At any rate, your intruding finger is also smack in the middle of Michigan's most famous trout country.

Named after *Thymallus arcticus,* the arctic grayling, the town sits astride the main branch of the Au Sable River. The river was once loaded with this lovely and too-easy-to-catch fish. They are long gone, thanks mainly to the logging boom of the late 1800s, which stripped the banks of Michigan's rivers, warming and fouling them. But overfishing didn't help either. The grayling were caught literally by the barrelful and shipped off to commercial markets.

Now the river is full of trout: browns, brookies, and some rainbows. And Grayling is Michigan's trout capital.

Never mind that Kalkaska, twenty-five miles to the west, hosts the annual Michigan Trout Festival. Although it has a statue of a giant brook trout—I would guess fifteen feet tall—in the center of town, it doesn't have the equivalent of an Au Sable River in the center of town, or anywhere nearby for that matter. So, sorry Kalkaska, you're a nice town and all, and I think it's hilarious and wonderful that you put on the trout festival—and I love the towering brookie—but you're not the *epicenter* of trout fishing in Michigan. Close, but not nearly close enough.

No, if you want to stand in the middle of Michigan's true trout fishing capital, stand at the corner of M-72 and Main Street in downtown Grayling. You're there. (And as long as you're standing there, you might as well walk up the street to Spike's for a cold one or three. The river flows right behind the bar.)

If you leave Grayling and head east on M-72 you'll run parallel to the main branch of the Au Sable, just to the north. And in a matter of minutes you'll begin passing access roads to the river, each of them holding special memories for generations of fly fishermen: Burton's Landing, Louie's Landing, Keystone, Thendara, Stephan Bridge, Wakeley Bridge. It's a stretch of the river rich in the history of trout angling.

Not long after you pass Wakeley Bridge Road, perhaps ten miles out of town, the highway drops slightly. Suddenly you find yourself, as though a curtain opened, on the lip of a broad, shallow valley, lush green hills rising in the distance. A few miles more, down in the valley, turn right on Canoe Harbor Road, a dirt road running off to the south. A mile or so down the road you'll come around a bend and discover a large sign in the woods to the left. I wish I would have written the words on that sign:

SPORTSMAN, SLOW YOUR PACE...AHEAD LIES THE FABLED LAND OF THE SOUTH BRANCH. HERE GENERATIONS OF FISHERMEN HAVE CAST A FLY ON ONE OF

THE GREAT TROUT STREAMS OF AMERICA. HUNTERS, TOO, HAVE ROAMED THESE HILLS IN THE SOLITUDE SO BOUNTIFULLY OFFERED. THE LAND IS RICH IN TRADITION AND STANDS READY TO RENEW YOUR SOUL. TREAD LIGHTLY AS YOU PASS AND LEAVE NO MARK. GO FORTH IN THE SPIRIT OF GEORGE W. MASON WHOSE GENEROUS GIFT HAS MADE THIS FOREVER POSSIBLE.

Deep in a wild area, high on a wooded bluff above the South Branch of the Au Sable, is a small chapel. It sits there in the forest, overlooking the river, on the east bank about midway between Chase Bridge and Smith Bridge. The river sparkles along for roughly twelve river miles between the two bridges. About five river miles below Smith Bridge it empties into the main branch of the Au Sable.

The little chapel is an unimposing thing, rough-hewn, open in the front. But there is something extraordinary about this structure, something unique, and that is this: In all those twelve miles of river it is very nearly the only man-made structure on either bank. Upstream there is one large dock, a rest area for canoeists. Beyond that, near Chase Bridge, there is a cabin on the east bank. Downstream, at Smith Bridge, there are a few houses and cabins on the upstream side of the bridge. But essentially, here's the better part of a trout stream—a great trout stream—that's just four hours north of one of the biggest cities in the nation, and its banks are still wild. How can this be?

This modern-day trout-stream miracle—and it is exactly that—is with us because of George Mason, the saint mentioned on the sign. Mason was an early Detroit industrialist and a passionate trout fisherman. The river of his passion was the South Branch.

In the early 1900s a chap by the name of Downey, along with several others, had a hunting and fishing club on the west bank of the river (just downstream from the present-day chapel). Downey ended up owning most of the forty-acre tracts that fronted the river for miles in each direction. He died in 1921 and the property passed through several hands, but Mason, who was often at the Downey camp, eventually acquired the land. He gave it to the state—and to trout fishermen forever—upon his death. As a condition of his bequest, he directed that the land never be developed. He also requested that the state maintain the little chapel he had built up on that bluff over the river.

Those twelve miles of woods and water are named in his honor. The Mason Tract.

If you follow the dirt road south, past the sign, you'll play tag with the river for many miles. Ten minutes or so past the sign and you'll come to a wire fence, a turn-in, and a big meadow sweeping down to the river. About halfway down the path to the river, in the meadow to the left, you'll find what remains of the foundation of Mr. Downey's old hunting and fishing club. Stone steps still lead to the river. A cement-and-rock seawall, though crumbling, still runs along the bank.

There's a little piece of shallow, fast water next to the meadow that is worth a few casts just before dusk on hot summer evenings. An occasional biggie will move into that oxygen-rich water to feed. I was standing just at the top edge of the riffle one hot August evening, changing flies, when I heard a deer walk into the quiet water upstream. Then I heard a tremendous splash. I turned and looked. The deer had collapsed in the center of the river. Only its head and neck showed, like a furry periscope. The deer lay there for a few moments, then rolled over on one side and began kicking it legs. Then it rolled over on the other side and did the same thing. It was certainly a commotion, water spraying everywhere. I wasn't sure what I was seeing there—a deer having some sort of attack? But the deer finally hopped to its feet, shook itself, and ambled upstream, drinking and pulling weeds from the river. It wasn't hard to figure out— the deer did what I wished I could have done. It cooled off and got away from the bugs.

Dogtown, Downey's, the Chapel, Baldwin's, Lower High Banks, High Banks, the Castle, the Hangar, Daisy Bend, Forest Rest. I've conducted business with the residents of all these historic pools and places.

One evening at Baldwin's, standing on the broad gravel bar where the creek comes into the river, I took two brook trout under the sweeper on the far side. The first fish measured exactly fifteen inches, the second $14\frac{1}{4}$, very big for Michigan stream brookies. Both fish took a Brown Drake. When the first fish lay at my feet in just inches of clear water, and I saw that it was a brook trout and not a brown,

I had a sudden and overpowering urge to kill that fish and mount it. It was incredibly beautiful, as brookies are, the white slashes on the fins gleaming in the evening light, the spots glistening. It was the only time I've ever had that urge and it lasted but a moment.

However, I do kill some trout from time to time, especially brook trout. I love to eat them, but I stick mainly to the pan-size variety. Those two large brookies I caught that evening were monarchs in the fiefdom of brook trout. And even though I had a momentary vision of that fifteen-incher hanging on the wall, I let them both swim away.

Any pilgrimage through the Mason Tract is not complete without a stop at the Castle, or what little is left of it. So one rainy afternoon I walked down to the old foundations with a friend from out of state. My friend Steve is not a fisherman, but he's a camper, hiker, birder, and all-around outdoor enthusiast, so a romp through the woods was just fine by him. He enjoyed the DNR's modest signboard, which shows old photos of the Castle and tells some of its story. And then we paced off the still-visible foundation, marveling that something so large could rise on the South Branch.

The Castle was built in 1930 by an early trout crazy named Durant. It was a monstrous fifty-room structure, standing there in a huge clearing by the river. Durant imported workers from Europe to help build this castle in the middle of nowhere. The workers lived in temporary cabins right on the property. Supplies were hauled in from Roscommon. Durant even carved an airstrip out of the woods so he could fly up from Detroit on weekends.

Strangely, the castle burned to the ground shortly after it was completed. No one knows exactly how it caught fire and all sorts of legends abound. But I once talked to a wonderful old fellow in Roscommon. Rollie, whose father worked on the project, told me he had been told that turpentine-soaked rags in a closet caught fire by spontaneous combustion. It was never rebuilt.

The foundations of the castle and hangar Durant built at the end of the landing strip are still there. Because it is such a popular stopping place for canoeists, the DNR built a large dock in the river there. The idea is to keep the idiots from destroying the bank and to keep the trash more or less centralized.

But there I was with my friend Steve, who was enjoying the tour, despite an on-again, off-again drizzle. We walked down to the canoe dock to check out the river and, lo and behold, a trout was rising directly across the stream. We watched and it continued to feed. It appeared to be a decent fish. So I skipped up the path to my truck and returned a few minutes later with my fly rod.

"He's still eating," said Steve.

I stripped out some line and popped a cast toward the opposite bank. Short.

"How do you know what bug it's eating?" asked Steve, getting into the swing of things.

I explained that I had a couple of good guesses, but didn't really know for sure. I also explained about generic flies like the #14 parachute Adams fixed to the end of my tippet.

Standing on the edge of the platform, I shot another cast across the river—narrow there—and the fly landed above the trout, floated down, and was promptly inhaled. Just like that.

There was a big splash as the surprised trout bolted for the overhanging brush on the far side. I knew right away it was a good fish. We managed to keep it out of brush, but things got a bit dicey when the trout made a frantic run downstream. Thankfully it didn't go far, because I was stuck on the dock and couldn't chase it.

The trout tired and we worked it back upstream. Steve was pretty excited and went for the fish.

"Gently," I said.

He was flat on his belly and a moment later came up with a still-wriggling handful of brown trout that turned out to be an honest sixteen inches. A lovely South Branch brown.

Steve gushed over it while I removed the fly. Then I lay on my belly and held the fish in the current, and shortly it scampered away.

"Wow, that was exciting!" Steve exclaimed. "There's nothing to it! It's so easy!"

"Nothing to it at all," I assured him.

I must have a dozen "favorite" places on this storied river. My son Jeff and I call one of our favorite spots simply "The Pool." It has no hallowed name, but it's a special place to us.

The river makes an S turn in a deep pine woods. At the bottom of the S there's a picture-perfect pool, one of those pools that looks trouty the moment you see it. The current pushes in against the bank and runs under a large cedar sweeper. The sweeper is just high enough over the water that you can actually get a fly in there. Just below the sweeper there's a marvelous back-eddy. A trout could lie there with his yap open and simply let the bugs pour down the hatch. And sometimes one does. When the little Olives come off, that pool lights up. I've counted as many as two dozen trout feeding in there and, during one magic afternoon, caught about that many without moving more than ten yards.

❖

The South Branch can cough up some big brown trout. The largest brown I've caught on the South Branch didn't come from the Tract. I caught it below Smith Bridge, well out of the Tract, upstream from a friend's cabin. It was 22½ inches of brown trout, taken on a Brown Drake, just at dusk.

But my second-largest trout did come from the Tract, and I'll tell you exactly where.

Just south of the Castle you'll find the old foundation of the Hangar, where Durant would park his plane during visits to his little construction project. Park there and follow the trail down the hill to the river. When you get to the river, you'll be right at or near a small island. Wade upstream about fifty yards, two or three bends, and where the river necks down, you'll see a logjam and a fairly deep pool on the west bank. On the east bank there's a handy tree trunk lying in the river, about love-seat size, where two fishermen can sit. That's the spot. You can't miss it, as they say.

I was there one June evening with a client. I was guiding then and this was a wading trip. The client was sort of a fussy old dude who didn't take direction very well but was okay once you got to know him.

That prettiest of mayflies, the Sulphur Dun, had been hatching every evening for about a week. They were really coming off on the mainstream, but I wanted to find some less crowded water. So there we were, in the hangar stretch of the South Branch.

The two of us were sitting on the log waiting for something to happen. I had floated through this pool many times, and several clients had taken some decent fish, but nothing spectacular.

I wasn't sure what would happen, but there are several different kinds of water there. If nothing happened in our pool, we could quickly move to a couple of other spots downstream.

The client was drinking a beer and smoking cigarettes and asking every five minutes if I thought this was a good spot. It is a silly question, really, to ask a guide. It's amazing how many people ask that question. Guides don't build a loyal following by taking their clients to crummy spots.

Lady Luck was on our side that evening. I had guessed well, and as dusk began to settle, little yellow Sulphurs made their appearance. Fish began to work immediately. I had the client wait for a few minutes, but a couple of good fish were rising and he was antsy. So we quietly worked our way into position and he began to fish.

It wasn't an easy place to throw a fly and he began having problems. He'd done all right earlier in the day, but some people seem to come unglued when they fish to specific trout and darkness is settling.

He lost two flies, one on the jam in the pool and the other in the brush behind us. I could have recovered the fly to our rear, but I didn't want to move.

There were now five or six fish working. My man finally got his act together and nailed a ten-incher in the tail-end of the pool. He was very pleased and surprised me by saying that he'd like to call it a day. I pointed across the way where a few fish were already rising again. He shrugged his shoulders and told me to give them a try if I wanted to.

What the hell. Although I never fish when I'm working, I always carry a rod. It's a spare really. And I do feel a little odd walking around in a trout stream without one.

One riser was sipping at the exact edge of a log. That fish made a big bubble every time he fed. Of the trout working there, that was the one that looked most interesting to me.

I made several dozen casts, but there was some goofy little current thing going on, and I had a hell of a time getting the fly to the edge of the log. Yet naturals were obviously floating in there.

I moved slowly upstream and my client moved over to our handy log and sat down. The pool shut down in a heartbeat, but I waited.

"You sure you don't want to try this?" I asked the client.

"Seriously, I'm done. I'm going to smoke a cigarette and watch you."

Sulphurs swarmed over the river and trout were feeding everywhere. They started again in our pool, including that interesting fellow tight against the log.

I worked out line and let a cast fall, checking it at the last second to give me some slack. The little Sulphur floated right in there, bumped the log, and—sip—disappeared.

The trout was very big and came boiling out from beneath that log and bolted downstream. I was right behind it and my client, Howard, was right behind me.

"This is a good fish! Do you want to play it?" I shouted.

"Hell no! You caught it, you play it!"

The fish made run after run, all downstream. The reel sang, that greatest of fishing music.

Initially there wasn't much I could do except hang on. The current runs pretty well there, especially in the straight stretch below the island.

That trout seemed to know his way around. The fish hightailed it for every piece of cover there was, first the logjam across from the island. I managed to put a stop to that. Then the trout headed straight for a submerged tangle of cedar logs just down from the island. By some miracle we got through there. Now there was a dash for that big old jam on the left at the bend. That's very still water there and I stayed well back, hoping the fish might stay there.

All this time my client was right behind me. Right then he decided to tell me that he'd left his rod back upstream. I had guided him five or six times and I'd never seen him as excited as he was now.

It was just dusk, a beautiful time on any trout stream, but particularly so on your favorite. A couple of whippoorwills started up somewhere; there were cedar waxwings dipping and soaring overhead.

The trout elected to stay in the quiet water near the big logjam. Eventually it became a question of who was going to wear out whom. This time, I won. I pumped the spent fish to the edge of the current where, sensing the faster water, it tried one last dash. But it was a feeble effort and I got my hand under its belly.

Howard put his flashlight on it even though it wasn't quite dark yet. It was a big, hook-jawed brown that measured just a shade over twenty inches. Howard had a point-and-shoot in his vest and insisted on a photo session. I held the trout in the water, out of the main current. A minute or two later it swam away.

"I must say, that was pretty damned exciting," said my client. "Well done." He extended his hand and I shook it. He was a pretty good dude after all.

I temporarily left him at the foot of the trail while I waded back up for his rod.

That was my biggest fish from the Tract. But a tiny fish, a couple of inches long, was just as special, if not more so.

For a couple of years I worked as a volunteer with the DNR's Au Sable system electro-shocking crew. Each year the Fisheries Division electro-shocked certain stretches of the various branches of the system. They surveyed the same areas from year to year, obviously for comparison purposes. The crew was glad to have a guide along as a volunteer. They found it interesting—I think—to get my view of the resource and the overall impression of my clients. (One thing I learned after working on the crew is that the Au Sable has plenty of good fish. But if you hang around in fly shops and eavesdrop, you'll know that fly fishermen have very active imaginations when it comes to the size of trout caught.)

By helping out, I felt I was giving a little something back to the thing that helped me earn a living. Since I was guiding, it didn't hurt of course to actually see where...but anyway.

We were shocking the river just above Chase Bridge. The three technicians on the electrodes were turning up a great number of fish and the action was fast and furious. Behind the three technicians with the probes were two guys with nets. They'd capture the stunned trout and pass them back to two guys wearing harnesses with a sort of mesh creel and a measuring board. Those two guys would measure the trout and toss them into a tub in the wooden barge that held the generator. The barge was guided by yet another technician. I was the tally man. The biologists with the measuring boards would shout a constant and rapid stream of "brown 10," "brook 6," "brook 5," "brown 13," "brown 8," "brook 4," and so on. Knowing that I guided, I think they made me the tally man because at that position there's almost no opportunity to watch what's going on. It's all you can do to keep up. The crew, of course, thought it was hilarious to shout "brown 29!" I fell for that just once.

But one afternoon, one of the crew, crusty old John Norcross, yelled "Hold it!" Everybody stopped. He turned and looked at me. I thought I was going to catch it again. Earlier in the day, when I was the barge man, I had inadvertently let the boat bump him when he was running one of the probes. He had chewed my ass in no uncertain terms. Later, one of the techs told me "You're not one of the crew until John chews you out for something. Welcome aboard."

But the veteran biologist wiggled his finger and said, "Come look at this." I waded over, as did the others, and there, in the fine mesh of his harness, was a gorgeous little fish, not three inches long, its back all the colors of a rainbow. "Do you know what this is?" he asked. I said no.

"It's a darter," he said. "We call it a rainbow darter."

We all looked. I couldn't believe the brilliance of its colors.

He held it up in the palm of his hand for me to see. "They're here in the river, but you'll never see one unless you do this kind of work," he said. And then he very gently let the gaudy little fish go. "Let's get back to work," he said.

I like to go to the South Branch in the evening. Up on the main stream and the North Branch cabin lights are coming on, telephones ring, televisions echo up and down the river. But on the South Branch, on Mr. Mason's stretch, the only sound is the river gurgling past my waders. It is the song of the South Branch.

11

RAIN FOREST TROUT

Across the table Tim was grinning. I grinned back. We were being hustled and we knew it. But it was a penny-ante hustle, small potatoes for fun, not for big Yankee dollars. In the next room the band started with the Spanish version of "Key Largo" (also the name of the joint), which would be repeated a few moments later in broken, but passable English.

Tim started to laugh and I couldn't help myself and laughed with him. Little Mischief, sitting next to me, gave me a rib-shot with her elbow. "Why you laughing?"

"Because you're up to your tricks again. That's why Tim and I call you Little Mischief."

"I not mischief!"

As if on cue, the waiter appeared and set cups of seviche in front of all of us.

I looked at Tim. "Did you order seviche?"

"I didn't order seviche," said Tim with a wink. "Did you order seviche?"

"I didn't order seviche. It must be a mistake."

Spoons were poised above cups. The aroma of the lime marinade in the cup in front of me with the chunks of cold, raw fish was doing a tap dance on my taste buds. There was absolute silence at the table, a minor miracle. Rosa, aka Little

Mischief, was watching me out of the corner of an eye. On the other side of me Maria politely put her spoon down.

Tim cleared his throat. "Well, maybe since it's already here. I mean, what the hell."

"Qué?" asked Maritza quietly.

I gazed off in the distance, looking grave. "It would probably look tacky if we tried to send it back."

"Give Americans a bad name," said Tim.

"Right." I looked at Little Mischief, who hadn't moved a muscle. "Okay. Hustled again, but okay."

There was a squeal of delight which set off a barrage of animated conversation, dark eyes flashing in the gloom of the old mansion-turned-nightclub in downtown San Jose. Our table was next to a tall, open bay window. Palms rustled outside. The scent of bougainvillea, with its large purple and red flowers, drifted around our cubbyhole. Long, black hair shimmered in the soft light. The bar was busy, con-versation a combination of several languages. There were American journalists, Costa Rican and American businessmen, (now a burst of German), and three Americans with sidewall haircuts looking very out of place in civilian clothes. Spoons clicked against cups of seviche.

"See, I no hustle you," said Little Mischief.

"I get it. Now that we've said it's okay, it's not a hustle anymore. What about last night?"

Rosa smiled. "Qué?"

"The pizza. Who ordered the pizza that Tim paid for?"

"Anna say she hungry for pizza last night."

"What about the singers? Who asked for the singers to come to the table?"

"Maria want to hear them."

"Oh, Maria. Maria didn't tell me she wanted to hear the singers."

"She say to me."

Tim is trying hard not to laugh. It was all so perfectly charming that we were trying to figure out how to keep it going for a while. I looked at Maria, who moved closer. I knocked down a shot of guaro and chased it with a pull on a bottle of Imperial. Guaro, the local poison, ran about ten cents a throw American and the beer, which was outstanding, was not much more. This was very inexpensive entertainment.

"So Anna was in the mood for pizza and Maria was in the mood for the singers," I continued.

"Sí!"

"Was I drunk or do I recall that the singers held their hats out after they sang?" I asked Tim.

"They passed the hat all right."

I gave Little Mischief a mini rib-shot in return. Maritza laughed, trying to follow.

"And I think we had to put some colóns in those hats."

"Right again."

I shook my head at Rosa. "Tim and I are going to start hanging out someplace else. You ladies are just too expensive."

Rosa said something to the others in rapid-fire Spanish. There was a chorus of "No, no!"

Later Tim and I split up, and Maria and I headed for the bus stop. On the way we stopped for a nightcap at a sidewalk cafe. Across the street, in the park, couples sat in the warm evening air. Down the street the film *Porkies* was playing at the theater. Tim and I had seen it earlier in the week and discovered that the audience was composed almost entirely of mothers and daughters who laughed and clapped and went "sssst! sssst!" during the ribald scenes. I had learned about this "sssst! sssst!" business the first week in town. "That means she wants to meet you!" said my new friend Keko.

Maria moved closer. I had been aware for several days that our friendship appeared to be moving to another plateau.

"I have the day off tomorrow," she said.

"I'm fishing. I'm going into the mountains with Keko."

"Always fishing."

"Yes."

"Always fishing," she said again. I could hear the resignation in her voice.

"Yes."

❖

In the morning I bought the International Edition of the *Miami Herald* and walked down the block to the sprawling central marketplace. It was early and *peónes* with loads of mangos, bananas, papayas, limes, and melons were entering the huge building. Inside, hundreds of small shops were getting ready for the day's business. I had taken to eating in some of the tiny cafes in the marketplace. Not only because they were cheap, but because the groceries were fresh from the countryside or the waters of either coast. The word "preservative" was not operative here.

After breakfast I sat on the hotel steps while the sun came up over the tops of the Cordillera Central, the mountain range that rings San Jose to the east. A few minutes later Keko's Jeep came around the corner.

We exchanged greetings, which nearly taxed the limits of my Spanish, and loaded my tackle. Keko Rodriguez spoke as much English as I did Spanish, but our shared passion for cold, clearwater streams had transcended the language barrier. During our trips into the mountains the phrase that stood my hair on end was "Muy grande truchas aquí!" Very large trout here!

Over the weeks the affable Keko and I had become friends. Keko owns one of the few tackle shops in Costa Rica that caters to freshwater fishermen. And he is one of a handful of anglers in the country who knows about the trout fishing high in the mountain rain forests. Keko had been nice enough to take time from the shop to take me into the mountains. Of course, Keko brought his tackle too. So I got to play hooky from a minor midlife crisis (I pawned the ring in a San Jose jewelry store) and Keko got to play hooky from the shop.

We drove southeast from San Jose, through the old town of Cartago, and through the valley of the Rio Orosi. Keko followed the Orosi, broad here, and then the road began to climb. We passed small dirt farms and huge *fincas* and Keko and I had an absolutely silly discussion about flies, understanding each other only because we were fishermen. Keko actually sells a pattern in his shop—one pattern— a brown, soft-hackle wet fly. He had one with him and insisted that it was the only fly I'd need. I responded by getting out my fly boxes because I enjoyed his amazed expression every time I opened them. I really don't carry that many flies, but to Keko, this was the worst and funniest case of overkill he had ever seen. He once made me understand that having all those flies was like going on a one-day bass fishing trip with five hundred crankbaits.

Up through coffee country we went; thousands and thousands of hectares of coffee plants surrounded us on the hillsides. Occasionally we passed a *peón* leading a burro laden with sacks, a sort of real-life Juan Valdez.

I held up a fly box and pointed to a row of Adams. "No," Keko said, laughing. I pointed to a parachute Brown Drake. He laughed and shook his head. I tried a Hendrickson. More laughter, still shaking his head. Then a Bivisible. He was nearly out of control. Still no. I indicated a row of tiny Blue-winged Olives. Ridiculous. This went on for a half-dozen more patterns until he finally held up the nondescript brown thing and said "Perfecto!"

The *fincas* gave way to the cloud forest and we saw the river only occasionally, deep in the gorge it had carved down the mountain. I put away the fly boxes because it was rather imperative that Keko keep both eyes glued on the road. High on the mountainside a narrow waterfall—a *cataracta*—dropped through the mysterious, deep-green forest to the river below. I could see bamboo down on the banks of the river; huge plants of elephant ear lined the roadside. Nothing in twenty years of trout fishing had prepared me for this. Most of us have an idea of what to expect when we finally arrive at a distant river. We come to equate trout with certain types of terrain. But this? This was a lost world, a black hole in the universe of trout. During the weeks to come I fished in the company of monkeys, three-toed sloths, a snake twice as long as I am tall, and birds too exotic for the books I had brought.

We drove into the clouds and I sensed Keko looking my way. "Magnífico, eh?" he said modestly.

"Muy bonito," I replied. Very beautiful. Keko did not take what he had for granted. It was one of the reasons I had grown to like him so much.

We continued up the mountain through the wet, glistening forest and I hoped for a glimpse of a quetzal, said to be the most beautiful bird in the world.

In 1920 the Costa Rican government stocked the upper reaches of more than eighty streams with Kamloops rainbows from our Washington State. The trout thrived. The *peónes* appreciated the generosity of their government and took up trout fishing. Because most of these streams were not wide it was a simple matter to stretch nets across, anchored on both banks. Upstream from the net the *peónes* would chop down a certain type of tree, the bark of which contains a mild poison. The tree would be pushed into the river and tied to the bank. Then the *peónes* went home and drank guaro while the nets filled with comatose rainbows. The local marketplaces were soon touting this wonderful addition to the fresh fish counter and the rivers were soon empty of trout.

There was a major restocking in 1976. The *peónes* once again cleaned out the more accessible rivers, but a wiser government also stocked streams far from the villages, some of them by helicopter. The trout flourished again in their mountain hideaways.

The road began to drop and we left the mist and were soon in a small valley. Moments later we stopped in front of a tiny adobelike home. Up the road was a bridge and I could see the Orosi beneath it, clear and swift. Keko indicated I should rig up. He went up to the house and spoke to the señora. I saw him pointing at the Jeep and gathered that he was asking if she would keep an eye on it. Then, true to form, Keko presented her with a sack of bread. Wherever we went, if there was a small favor to ask, or permission to be granted, Keko always had a bag of fresh-baked bread. This wasn't bribery; it was a simple thank-you. And as I watched, it was apparent that the satisfaction was in the giving rather than knowing someone would be watching the Jeep. Far from any market, this peasant woman was pleased to receive a few loaves of bread baked that morning in the city. Sure, the deal worked both ways, but I had the feeling that even if someone stole the Jeep, it would be okay as long as that woman, on that lonely road high in the mountains, had her bread.

It was then that the little señorita appeared. For the second time that day I was unprepared for what I saw. Before me stood the most beautiful young woman I had ever seen. She had come like a ghost, moving on bare feet, and she stood now, shyly smiling at the *norteamericano*. Her white smock shifted in concert with her sparkling raven hair, a child of mountain breezes. Perhaps thirteen, maybe fourteen, she already had that easy, feminine grace and wonderful smile that come early to Latin women. Untouched by the society of the shopping mall, boom boxes, video games, and other forms of madness, an innocence radiated from her that is gone from most American kids at a very early age these days.

I followed Keko along the river heading upstream from the bridge, thinking about my Little Vision (as I had already named her) but also wondering about the Orosi and its wild rainbows.

The river was thirty to forty feet wide and ran like a silvery snake through the rain forest. There was no path and we often hiked some distance away from the river and then angled back to it. The forest gave way to an old coffee field and there, on the other side, at the edge of the forest again, was the river. It was very narrow here, not more than ten feet, and in the center was a large rock. Keko pointed to the rock and said that next to it there was a *muy grande trucha*. He indicated that we would begin here and work downstream where the river had more width. We would split up, leapfrogging each other from pool to pool. But first, he wanted me to try here. I gave him some jazz about the big one that was supposedly by the boulder, but he smiled and insisted it was so. I asked him if he had any idea how many others had fished here. As far as he knew, no one else. Only he and his son.

For all the kidding about flies, Keko actually liked the contents of my meat box: Woolly Buggers, Muddlers, Marabous, etc.—all large. He approved of the Black Matuka I tied on.

Staying back from the bank and muttering about *muy grande truchas,* I cast the fly above the rock and worked it down. I put cast after cast on all sides of the rock without a nudge. Keko urged me on, but finally I suggested that he chuck his spinner in there. He winced, but I insisted.

I watched the spinner hit the water just above the rock with a nice splash. Keko took a couple of turns on the reel and then yelled when a good-sized rainbow materialized like a rocket out of nowhere, slashed at the spinner and missed. Keko happily doled out a full measure of *I told you so* and insisted I try again.

This was an improbable scene. Here I was, on the margin of an old coffee plantation, high on a mountain surrounded by a Cimmerian forest full of extraordinary noises, next to a man with whom I really couldn't converse. Like two Englishmen sharing a beat, we were politely trading the pool, pausing only when a cloud came by to wet us and obscure everything. The clouds not only went over us, but around us and below us.

I changed to a bright streamer and did my own version of chucking it in there. Here came the rainbow, whacked the fly, tossed it, and disappeared.

"Eiyeeee!" exclaimed Keko.

We rested the pool and tried again, but didn't move the fish. It looked to have been about four pounds, slightly larger than the average Costa Rican rainbow. Most of the trout ran two or three pounds, not large, but very strong and quick, probably because of the constant, fast current.

I left Keko, who wanted to try a pool upstream, slipped into the river, and followed it into the gloom. The water was very cold and strewn with large boulders. The stream widened almost immediately and shafts of sunlight came through the canopy overhead. Huge ferns, elephant ear, and bamboo lined the banks. Vines climbed the trees and everything else that grew to any height. I came down with a bad case of having to see what was around the next bend and passed some choice-looking pools as I moved along. I rounded one bend and there was a bankful of orchidlike flowers, hundreds and hundreds, pale-blue and white. I picked a blue one and attached it to my vest. Feeling sporty, I lit a cigar.

Ahead of me the river tumbled over a ledge and I got out, circled the pool, and angled below it. I tossed the fly into the base of the miniature waterfall, stripped once, and was onto a nice rainbow. Again I was surprised at the strength of the fish. The rainbow tailwalked nearly the width of the pool and shot back under the little waterfall. I put some pressure on the rod and the trout was out in the pool again, jumping like no tomorrow, paying homage to its Washington State progenitors. It tired and I lifted the little cane rod and slid the fish onto the gravel. It was about three inches longer than the twelve-inch wrap on the rod. I unhooked it and sent it back to its waterfall.

I missed many more than I caught. The least bit of slack line or hesitation in setting the hook and those rainbows were gone. I fished too fast, but I was captivated by this mysterious river and wanted to see all of it. For me, the best part of trout fishing is where you end up doing it. That's what grabs the soul, or at least mine. I thought about the Firehole with its steampots and geysers, the Bow with its eagles soaring over the towering bluffs, the George flowing through tundra alive with caribou, beaver ponds hidden deep in the pine and birch forests of northern Michigan.

And now this. And right then I knew for certain that I was right where I needed to be. It had been many months, but the memories of the senseless, bitter fights were still too fresh. The end came when, after not speaking to me for a couple of days, she dressed up one night, took the ice cube trays from the refrigerator, and drove off. Without so much as a word. The ice cube trays. I kid you not. I was out the door with my fly rods in less than ten minutes.

I fished down to the bridge where I lingered in the lower pools and finally Keko came along. He had kept some trout and we laid them on a huge leaf of elephant ear and I photographed them. Keko broke out a bottle of rum and some sandwiches and we had a little tailgate party, right there on top of that mountain in the middle of nowhere. A little later the episode of the ice cube trays was a more distant memory.

Over the coming weeks, whenever Keko could take time away from the shop, we fished more of these rain forest rivers. I especially remember the Rio Poas, with its head-waters near the top of the volcano of the same name. It was smaller than the Orosi, with descending pools separated by little waterfalls, each prettier than the next.

Nearly every evening Tim and I would head for the Key Largo and a rendezvous with Maria and Little Mischief. The place was a hangout for journalists and the U.S. consulate staff and a good place to hear the latest on what was happening elsewhere in Central America. Later Tim and I would walk the city and have dinner in one of the open-air restaurants, making sure we had a table where we could watch the señoritas pass by. We had our favorites for this, particularly one place on a corner across from one of the small parks. This was a busy intersection with a bus stop and the parade of señoritas was endless. One evening Tim got the old "ssssst! ssssst!" business from the window of a bus and chased it two blocks. I had a glimpse of her and would have done the same thing.

Tim had recently been through a situation similar to mine, but with less acrimony. Still, things tended to get out of hand at night. One evening we got a little plastered and made friends with a four-man marimba crew. The guys would play like hell in one cantina and pass the hat. Then we would shoulder the huge instrument and carry it down the street to another bar. One evening we celebrated Tim's birthday and he got extra smashed. With a little encouragement, he took over the middle section of the marimba and played some Dave Brubeck. The other three guys picked up on the tunes and the audience went crazy. These musicians worked one section of town and in the evenings we could usually find them by following our ears.

Maria was patient and attentive—and beautiful, a miniature Sophia Loren. She worked for one of the travel agencies and, when I wasn't fishing, we'd often meet for lunch near her office and then again later at night. But we both knew that, inevitably, the day would come. It was the best of times, it was the worst of times.

Through all of this there lurked the legend of Cerro de la Muerte, the Mountain of Death. At its base, deep in a gorge, flows the Rio Orosi, far from the headwaters I had fished. It is said that this stretch holds the biggest rainbows in all of Costa Rica, although no one has ever fished for them. The only way to find out would be to go straight down the Mountain of Death through the rain forest. We talked about it a lot. Someone went down there once to find the river and never came out. Keko wouldn't take us, but thought maybe he could find someone.

Some day.

12

THE SEARCH FOR
ROBINETTE CRUSOE

The quiet girl from California looked irritated. You could see it even in the dim light of the lanterns. Two medical students, male and female, had arrived early in the afternoon on the bus from Alajuela. Discovering a fellow Californian, they assumed they had the makings of a merry group of three. The medical students looked silly in their baggy shorts and surgical uniform tops as they trailed her from beach to bar and back again all day.

I had spent the afternoon in the bar watching the comings and goings of this strange trio. The owner of the bar, Hernan, was mighty taken with what the tall, quiet one's beachwear barely hid. I had first seen her a few evenings before, and there was just enough pain in those eyes to get my attention. In the days that followed she would nod, but seldom spoke.

Hernan was also the mayor of Quepos, the little village ten minutes up the beach. In his dual role as mayor and bartender, Hernan had an opinion on everything. I got on his good side early by telling him that he had, in *my* opinion, the best bar I had ever patronized "in my entire life." Certainly in the top five, I said. And I meant it. It was a thatched-roof affair, open on three sides, with a bar at one end and tables scattered around. We were surrounded by jungle. Twenty yards away, beyond a stately file of palms, was *El Pacifico*. There wasn't one iota of tourist clack anywhere to be seen. Honest bars are a vanishing species and I was overjoyed to find this one in a distant place. But these days that's certainly where they're most likely to be found. Once tourists start showing up—anywhere—the gimmicks and fakery are never far behind. Watching the smelly medical students, I feared for the future of Hernan's.

I had been up in the mountains in central Costa Rica fishing for trout with my friends Tim and Keko. After a few weeks of climbing around in the rain forest, Tim and I decided a couple of weeks at the beach wouldn't hurt.

Hernan was fascinated by this business of fly fishing, and I spent a pleasant afternoon giving a somewhat fuzzy edition of matching the hatch, right through to tight loops. Hernan was a rapt student and extracted promises of a casting demonstration the next day. I had brought along my heaviest rod and thought I might find some cove, and fish off the beach. The eight-weight was a little light for serious salt water, but nothing ventured, nothing gained.

For his part, Hernan did a good hour or so on rip tides and clearly considered himself an authority. As a rip-tide novice, it was my turn to be a fascinated student.

Tim had spent the day on the beach and had later gone up the road to visit friends.

I had moved about five yards all day, from the bar to one of the tables. Hernan's Dalmatian, Rice and Beans, lay at my feet. Rice and Beans had it made and I told him so several times. After all, he spent virtually every day in a bar on an exotic beach. As nearly as I could tell, his only task was to bark at the occasional appearance of the monkeys that would come tribelike through the treetops to the ocean's edge and scream and throw stuff on hapless passersby.

I sat in the pleasant gloom trying to hear the ocean over the know-it-all yapping of the med students, who, like first-year anythings, were already seasoned veterans and anxious to prove it. The quiet one was clearly annoyed, and I wondered why she didn't tell the two idiots to take a hike.

Hernan came over to my table and sat down. "She will dismiss them soon and then you can make your move," he said in a low voice.

I wasn't so sure about any move and said so.

"She will be a good one, that one!" insisted Hernan.

I said that I wasn't interested in gringo women. I told Hernan that I liked his country's pretty *ticos*.

"Yes, of course. But you wouldn't turn it down would you?"

The pretty one left with her entourage and was back five minutes later, alone. Hernan left and she sat down and we talked for several hours. She had come to this far-away beach to forget something in her recent past and I was happy to lend an ear. Talked out and grateful, she left well after midnight.

I was about to leave when Hernan came over. "No luck?"

"No effort. She's got enough problems."

"A little crazy?"

"Just sad. If she'd been just a little crazy I might have been a little interested."

We sat there in the dark and listened to the Pacific roll onto the beach. I was tapped-out on beer and guaro, the local kerosene, and asked Hernan to bring me a Jack Daniels. I had spotted the rare bottle behind the bar. I knew it would be expensive, but it had come a long way from the holler. To my surprise the drink was on the house.

"It is my pleasure," said Hernan as I thanked him. After a while he said, "Do you know the story of Robinson Crusoe?"

"Sure."

"There is a gringo woman who lives like him on an island in the Rio Naranjo up in the foothills of the mountains. She lives in a grass shack and eats fruits, and fishes for machaca. The river is said to boil with them." *Boil with them?*

❖

The next day at noon Tim and I waited for *El Bala* (The Bullet), the bus that would take us to the village of Londres. Hernan said the village was on the river and thought that someone there would know about the Canadian woman who lived on the island.

We waited at the village square. The scent of the ocean came on the wind. Quepos had once been a shrimping port, but the shrimpers had moved up the coast to Puntarenas. There were a number of people waiting for El Bala. Most had empty baskets, and it was apparent that they had come down from the hills to sell their goods. One dour old man sat on a crate that held two chickens. From the look of them I guessed that they hadn't made the cut and were being sent home to fatten up.

The Bullet finally pulled up to the shed that served as the bus station. Like many buses throughout Latin America, this one was garishly painted. The driver's compartment was decorated with tassels and fringe. The words "El Bala" were painted on both sides and on the front and back in large, silver script. The driver eyed my rod tubes and vest.

Several dusty hours later The Bullet chugged into Londres (Spanish for London, if you can imagine), barely into the foothills of the mountains we had flown over in twenty minutes a week earlier.

Londres turned out to be a crossroads with a cantina on one corner and a banana shed on the other. The banana shed had a pool table in a separate room that appeared to be in pretty good shape.

Tim and I went into the cantina and asked the woman behind the makeshift bar about the gringo woman. The señora knew of her and pointed up the road and said "dos kilometers." I had two quick Imperial beers while Tim tried to sort out the directions. The señora seemed to lack specifics and I wondered if it was intentional. Anyone looking for the woman would logically stop in the cantina. I certainly wasn't there to disrupt her lifestyle. I merely wanted her to show me the Magic Kingdom of the Machaca, that place in the river said to *boil* with them.

My rip-tide expert, Hernan, had never caught a machaca, but he had seen them caught on handlines. He said they were tremendous fighters and held his hands about two feet apart when I asked him how big they got. Since he wasn't a fisherman I tended to believe him. Because he had taken my clinic I asked him if he thought they could be caught on flies. "No problema," he assured me, grinning.

We started up the road, which appeared to be angling away from the river. We had crossed the Naranjo on the outskirts of the village. There it was about seventy-five yards wide, and shallow. It was also very muddy. It reminded me of some of the streams I had fished in northern Ohio as a kid, except the Naranjo was much larger.

We walked for about an hour and not once did we see the river. The road was straight and climbing slightly. I was beginning to get the feeling that we either didn't get the directions right or the señora was under instructions to send strangers some other way.

About then we heard a shout and a guy came out of a shed up on the hillside. He was a local, but spoke near-perfect English and was overjoyed to find two gringos strolling along the road in front of his shack.

Ramon turned out to be the local jewelry maker. He wore shorts, and numerous samples of his work around his neck. It was nice stuff, and he used stones that he found locally. The shed was his workshop, and every so often he would take The Bullet down to Quepos to sell his work. He had traveled and had been to the U.S.

Yes, he knew how to find the Canadian woman, but here was a man thirsty for company and there was no getting away for a while. He was curious (like everyone we met) about our fishing, and said that there had been a big storm in the mountains the night before and that the river was very high and fast. And no, we hadn't walked far enough. We should walk a little farther and there would be a fence with a gate. Go through the gate and follow the path to the river.

"Where is the river?" I asked.

He pointed. "It's about half a kilometer away in the valley. You can't see it from the road."

Finally we got away and walked some more. No fence, no gate. We were standing in the middle of the dirt road wondering what to do when a little kid came out of a hut. Tim, whose Spanish is pretty good, was navigator by default and went to work on the kid. The little boy pointed back down the road in the direction from which we had just come. I shook my head and was fairly certain that the woman lived the way she did because she liked her solitude. I even had a momentary vision of Hernan telling terrifically funny stories across the bar about the two gringos he sent on the wild-goose chase.

It was then that Tim had the Big Idea. He reached into his pocket and brought out some coins. The kid's hand moved at the speed of light, but Tim was quicker. He jingled the coins, and it was clear to me that they would change hands only when the grass shack was in sight. The kids took off at a good clip down the road. We were right after him.

"Brilliant, Ryan," I said.

"Money talks."

The kid turned off the road between two old posts. There was a rusted hinge hanging from one of the posts. "The gate," I said.

Tim pointed at a piece of rusty wire lying in the weeds. "This must be the fence," he said.

There was a path of sorts and it dropped from the road in a gradual descent to what was obviously bottom land. Ten minutes later we entered a treeline. Twenty yards more and there was the Rio Naranjo, swift and muddy. There was an island directly across from us. In a clearing on the island was a grass shack.

The temporary leader of our expedition stuck his hand out and Tim paid off. The boy disappeared, a little quickly I thought.

A heavy steel cable stretched between a tree on the island and a nearby tree on our side of the river. Below it was a small platform suspended from trolley wheels which rode the cable.

Tim and I watched the island for some sign of the woman. Except for the hiss of the Naranjo, it was very quiet.

"What do you think?" asked Tim.

I didn't know what to think. There were all sorts of possibilities. At one end of the spectrum I envisioned a grateful fellow *norteamericano* starved for news, and that we would spend the day in pleasant conversation, perhaps sipping a high-octane, exotic refreshment she brewed herself. At the other end I had visions of a reclusive nut case blowing me off the platform with a 12-gauge from halfway across the river. Possibilities aside, what was propriety here? I had never winched myself over to a grass shack on an island in the middle of a river. What would Miss Manners suggest?

"Hell, let's go over," I heard Tim saying.

I hopped up on the platform and, swaying above the boulder-strewn river, pulled myself across. "Hello the island!" I yelled as I neared the other side. There was no answer and, after I jumped off, I sent the trolley back to Tim. Tim came across and yelled and still no answer.

The shack had three sides and a thatched-type roof. Two hammocks hung suspended inside. There was a small table and a couple of stools. Various cooking utensils were scattered here and there. By God, it was spartan. Nearby was an outhouse of sorts.

The island lady was obviously elsewhere. Paths led from the clearing in several directions.

"Maybe she's picking fruit somewhere," offered Tim.

Or maybe she's handlining that hot machaca hole, I thought. I couldn't get "boil with them" out of my head.

We followed a couple of the trails, discovering that they led to the river on the far side of the island. One path ended at what looked to be a fishing hole.

"You want to try it?" asked Tim.

The only way to have worked a fly in there would have meant getting in the river upstream. That was clearly impossible with the river so high and swift. As I stood there watching the river I suddenly had a very unpleasant thought. The island lady wasn't on her island and I said so to Tim.

"How do you know?"

"Because the cart was on the *mainland* side. If she would have been here the cart would have been on *this* side."

"If she comes back and discovers..."

"She might freak."

Tim and I hustled back to the shack, took another look around, hopped the trolley, and pulled ourselves back to the mainland. The trolley dipped perilously close to the mad, muddy river.

"Well, shit," said Tim as we disembarked.

"Maybe we'll catch her walking along the road." But I felt like Tim, maybe worse, because the chances of catching machaca were going up in smoke. At this point I didn't even know what they looked like, despite Hernan's attempted description.

We walked back to Londres and sat in the sun outside the cantina and drank beer. The Bullet wasn't due back until mid-evening and there wasn't a thing to do except drink, which—in lieu of fishing for machaca with the abstruse Canadian—was fine with me. I got up and went inside the cantina and came back out with a beer and a water glass filled with guaro. Tim laughed. "Right on. There's no point in getting up every five minutes."

"That's the way I see it."

Mindlessly I began to rummage around in my vest. My junk pocket overflowed with old cigar wrappers, several dead lighters, a broken compass, and a half-eaten granola bar.

There was a commotion across the street. Several banana pickers were starting to shoot pool and motioned for Tim and me to join them. I stayed right where I was, but Tim went and I knew that the amigos were in for a big surprise. As a designer and photographer, Ryan has always had a good eye. I played pool with him in high school and he was one of the finest amateur shots I'd ever seen.

I continued to empty vest-pockets, something I had not done in a long time. From the inside left-hand pocket came some snarled tippet spools (I need a better system than this, I said to myself for the sixty-millionth time) and a crumpled-up, somewhat-official-looking form. I began to discard it, but my curiosity was aroused. I uncrumpled it and what did I find? A parking ticket. A parking ticket from the police department of Troy, Michigan. This was too much. A parking ticket had followed me 2,500 miles to another continent. In my fishing vest.

I read the ticket: Parking in a no-parking zone, Chrysler Financial Building, Crooks Road, and then a smudged date, May 2, 198-something, $5.00 payable to City of Troy, Traffic Dept.

About that time I was dating a woman who worked in the Chrysler Building and she was crazy about fly fishing. Let's see, May 2? Maybe there were still some Hendricksons? Maybe I was so pumped to get to a trout stream that I picked her up from work one Friday night and was already wearing my vest and waders when I met her in the lobby? Whoa!

I took a pull on the guaro, chased it with the beer, and considered a course of action. Perhaps I should march into the constable's little office in Quepos, hand him the ticket and five bucks and say, "Put this on the computer and zap it off to Michigan. I can't have this on my conscience." Or better still, I'll give it to Hernan late tonight and have him use his pull to "fix it." Conspiracy on an international level! Hernan will be thrilled.

The ticket ended up, of course, in the pile with the cigar wrappers and other junk. I was, after all, a few thousand miles from home (which was then in Brooklyn anyway) and not a soul knew where I was. I had no driver's license, no checking account, no nothing. No computer system short of the CIA's could find me. Except for my passport, I had no official ties to the real world. It was a startling, wonderful thought in an age when Americans have lost all of their privacy.

But I had escaped the system, at least for now. The señora behind the bar became an unwitting accomplice when she took my trash, including the parking ticket, and threw it away.

A vest with a parking ticket and an empty grass shack; it had been a day of mysteries, and suddenly I decided to go machaca fishing, muddy river or not. There was much laughter coming from the one-table pool hall, and it sounded as though the Brooklyn Kid was having a great time.

I walked down to the river and hiked upstream from the bridge, feeling a little foolish, actually. It occurred to me that I had become programmed by clear-running trout streams. So what if the Naranjo was muddy. If there were machaca here they had to eat, sometime.

I found a large pool just out from the bank where the current seemed to be slower because of a rocky bar upstream. I hopped onto a handy rock just off the bank, cut back my tippet, and tied on a big Woolly Bugger. It had an olive body with black hackle and a thick, black marabou tail. As I gazed over the muddy pool, I wished I had some Dr. Juice with machaca hormones or whatever they put in that stuff.

Just as I was about to cast, a young *peón* dressed only in shorts walked out to the end of the bar above me. He had a familiar-looking bottle of shampoo, and he knelt on the end of the bar, dipped his head in the river, and lathered his hair. Soap bubbles began to drift through the pool. Off in the distance a woman yelled. The boy waved an arm. He heard me strip line, looked my way, and shook his head. I grinned and nodded. Mothers.

A flock of brightly colored but unfamiliar birds zigged by as I let my first cast go, and the Woolly Bugger landed in the Head & Shoulders bubble line. I mended upstream and stripped in. I probably cast a couple of dozen times when I had an incredibly savage strike. I didn't have to worry about easing the slack through my fingers to get the line on the reel; the slack line disappeared in a second and then the fish was out of the pool and into the main current.

Upstream I heard the kid yelling "Amigo! Amigo!" At first I didn't pay any attention, but he kept it up and I looked upstream. He was pointing across the river. A three-toed sloth hung from a branch in a tree on the opposite bank. And I thought he was cheering for the gringo fisherman.

For a few moments it was a standoff and then the fish took off downstream. That turned out to be perfect because I was able to lean into the fish and angle it back into the pool at the lower end. About five minutes later, I was able to drop the tip, take in line, and pump the fish toward me. But every time I got it in the shallows it took line out with powerful surges. Finally I muscled it up to the rock and it bolted again. At the far side of the pool it jumped in a spray of water. I still didn't know what I had on, but I was having a hell of a good time. My little buddy from upstream was with me now and he kept watching the rod. Later I learned that he had seen plenty of fish caught, but only on handlines.

Once again I worked the fish back to the rock. In retrospect I should have gotten off the rock and slid the fish onto the bank. But because I was anxious to see it, I knelt on the rock and tried to work the fish in close. In the murky water I could occasionally see glimpses of it. When I thought it was played out, I lifted the rod and followed the leader down toward the fly. And then it occurred to me: I didn't know if the fish—if it was a machaca—had teeth. Or spines? I didn't know the Spanish word for teeth, so I tapped my small amigo on the shoulder, smiled my best Bucky Beaver smile, pointed to my teeth and then down to where I could just see the silhouette of the fish. The lad understood perfectly. Standing in water up to his knees next to my rock, he bowed slightly from his waist toward the fish and then grinned hugely. He looked up briefly, his eyes large, the smile frozen in place, and turned back to where the leader entered the water, still grinning.

I slowly worked my fingers down the leader and thought that this is how weird stories about Americans get started. For years to come in Londres, they'll be talking about the strange gringo who insisted that you should smile at the fish while catching him.

When I thought I was close, I lifted the leader and was rewarded with a sharp pain in my right thumb. I dropped the rod on the rock and grabbed my right hand.

The Woolly Bugger was lodged in the end of my thumb, not past the barb, thanks for small favors. Next to the rock, I saw a tail disappear in the murk.

That was it. It was not for me to catch a machaca or to meet Robinette Crusoe.

I went back to the cantina and sat in the dust outside with my back against the warm adobe, my eyes closed, the sun in my face. I made hand prints in the fine, warm dirt. Banana palms rustled in the breeze. Across the road I heard Tim exclaim, "No eight-ball I ever played had that rule!" But he was laughing and so were his new friends. The señora came out with a beer. Except for a sore thumb, I was a number ten on the happiness scale.

Eventually El Bala carried us back to Quepos where, late that night, I updated Hernan on the day's events. He had news, too. The noisy medical students had left. The quiet one from California had moved on as well.

"She said to thank you and to say goodbye and this is on her," said Hernan as he set a shot of Jack Daniels on the bar along with a beer.

That night I dreamed about the island lady. In my dream she looked like Maureen O'Sullivan. Cheetah was there, too.

13

❖

JACK'S HOLE

W̲e were in a stretch of the Alagnak called the Braids, some distance upstream from the lodge. Here the river broke up into several channels, and it was here that my guide, Jack, had named a pool after himself—Jack's Hole.

I instantly liked Jack for a variety of reasons. For showing me his own, personal pool for one thing—even though he almost never got to fish it. And what a pool it was. It had formed below a little island where one of the channels took a left turn over a gravel bar. Jack's Hole was about thirty yards long and ten yards wide and deep enough that you could only see the bottom when the sun was just right. Jack's Hole almost always had a couple of big rainbows in it.

I also liked Jack because he didn't think it was silly to knock off fishing for the Alagnak's big rainbows for a while and fish for something that had been wiped out in my home state of Michigan. I thought it was only proper to finally fish for a fish whose name appeared on every piece of mail I received. It always struck me as odd that I lived near Grayling, Michigan, and had never seen the fish in the flesh. (That's not *entirely* true. I had never seen a *wild* grayling in the flesh. Michigan's DNR planted grayling in nearby

Neff Lake and in various other waters of the state. I actually caught some of those Neff Lake grayling, right off the beach at the campground the year after they were stocked. I never caught any more after that and I don't know how they made out elsewhere in the state. Someone told me the fingerlings were from Montana. It seemed unsettling to be catching Montana grayling near Grayling, five minutes south of the Au Sable River which, before Michigan's logging boom wiped them out around the turn of the century, used to be one of the most prolific grayling streams in North America. So I had never actually caught a *wild* grayling.)

I also liked Jack because he didn't mind if I didn't fish for salmon. I caught one the first day to please him, but explained that I could catch all of these I wanted back in the good old Wolverine State (which has no wolverines). I was interested in rainbows. Big ones.

I also liked Jack because he carried a five-shot, stainless steel 12-gauge shotgun everywhere we went. It was the noise, he explained, that would scare the huge brown bears away. (Guide's joke: "The first four shots are for the bear," says the guide. "What's the fifth shot for?" asks the sport. "To put you out of your misery," says the guide.)

I also liked Jack because all he did was roll his eyes when I told him that I had just come from shooting a video about tournament bass fishing. It was true. Barely forty-eight hours before my plane landed in King Salmon on the Alaska Peninsula, I had been aboard a bass boat on the Lake of the Ozarks with Denny Brauer, who was flippin' and pitchin' for our camera. And just before that I'd been with Guido Hibdon, who had managed to catch an outsized bass for the camera on light line and a small jig using his finesse fishing techniques. The video would also feature George Cochran on topwater fishing, Rick Clunn on crankbaits, and Larry Nixon on wormin' and jiggin'. Five of the top names in professional bass fishing.

Right then I wished I had a flippin' rod, a notion that a year or two earlier I would have found incredible. But it really was a textbook flippin' situation. I was in a side channel not far from Jack's Hole trying to put my flesh fly (more about this tasty pattern later) into a promising-looking little pocket tight to the bank. A brown bear had chosen that spot to enter the river quite recently, and the grass on the bank was flattened out well over the water. A tangle of branches guarded the upstream end of the pocket.

The idea was to get the fly not only under the over-hanging brush but, better still, back under the bank, which was clearly undercut. Visions of Brauer danced in my head. I had watched him flip jigs several *feet* beneath boat docks on the Lake of the Ozarks with only inches of clearance be-tween the dock and the water. The first time he did it the collective eyeballs of the camera crew nearly popped out of their sockets. We had just seen a fishing lure redefine some law of physics. Knowing, of course, that we were impressed, he would also let his bait (a lure in bass fishing lingo) dangle about a foot beneath his rod tip. He'd then give the rod a little shake and the bait would do sort of a circular, double loopty-loop around the tip and then arc out over the water and land about one-sixteenth inch from a piling or in a hole in the lily pads the size of a dime.

I was actually about ready to forget the spot but thought, what the hell, why not try to slop one in there? So I sort of side-armed the fly line along the water. The fly somehow shot beneath the grass, landed with an audible "plop," and there was a tug followed by an explosion. A big rainbow came charging out of the little pocket and was twenty-five yards downstream before I could say flippin' and pitchin'.

This was my fourth or fifth Alagnak rainbow and I was still unprepared for how spectacularly they fight. When you finally land one you notice how muscular they are, which helps to explain their championship performance. There's nothing soft about them; they're hard as a rock. I suppose they get that way because they eat a lot of meat. Meat in the form of dead salmon and salmon eggs. They also eat mice and other small critters that might fall into the drink. But when the salmon are running the rainbows have a gargantuan supply of high protein. They eat both the salmon eggs and the decomposing bodies of the salmon. As the salmon disintegrate, chunks of flesh break loose and drift with the current, easy pickings for the rainbows.

My rod was vibrating and bent into that wonderful curve we dream about and write about, thanks to a lucky cast and a flesh fly. The flesh fly is simply a fluff of grayish white marabou tied to the hook. Drifted in the current, it looks just like a chunk of decomposed salmon. While this may sound less than tasty to you and me, to a rainbow it's a steak dinner of the first magnitude. Perhaps a smallish filet mignon, maybe a big porterhouse. Relatively speaking, I would say that the guides at Katmai Lodge tie them New-York-strip-steak size. As you might imagine, they are fast and easy to tie. A group of Brits had been in camp the week before and one of the guides said several of them had been properly horrified by the flesh fly. I wasn't surprised—the fly is no Jock Scott—but still, fishing for carp with maggots is big sport in merry old England. Come on.

I managed to keep the rainbow out of the main channel. For about ten minutes it was a standoff—all I could do was hang on. The fish made several heart-stopping runs, the line singing through the guides, and then bulldogged ferociously and refused to budge.

There was a gravel bar where my channel joined another, and when the fish finally tired I was able to coax it into shallow water, where it made another short but wild run, spraying water as it shot across the bar. I pumped it back and there it was, gasping in the inches-deep, clear water. The fish was an honest six or seven pounds, wonderfully spotted, and had of course a gorgeous red slash on each flank.

Denny Brauer had told me what to expect. He had taken off for Alaska during a break one year in the tournament schedule, hired a plane, and popped around Alaska fishing for everything, but remembering the rainbows more than anything. We were sitting in his boathouse drinking beer during a break in the shooting and his eyes sort of glazed over when he started talking about Alaskan rainbows. "Jim, you're not gonna believe how they fight."

"Better than a bass?" I jokingly asked.

"I'd say," he said smiling. "But they don't pay as good." We all laughed, including the camera crew. Brauer has won hundreds of thousands of dollars on the tournament circuit, not to mention the steady money from companies that sponsor him. (His colleague, Larry Nixon, was the first pro to go over the million-dollar mark in tournament winnings.)

I held the handsome, big rainbow in the current while it got its wind back. Jack was there and we watched together as the fish suddenly shot from my hand.

"It looked mean," I said to Jack.

"They do look mean, don't they?"

We have rainbow trout in Michigan just as big but they're called steelhead. These Alaskan rainbows are *resident* fish, "regular" rainbows except that they can easily weigh eight or nine pounds. An alleged eleven-pounder was taken while I was there.

The Alagnak is a tundra river fed by Nonvianuk Lake, which is within the boundary of Katmai National Park and Reserve. It empties into Kvichak Bay, a small arm of immense Bristol Bay, part of the Bering Sea.

This is country that makes you wish you had been born at least a hundred years earlier, although it's not much changed even now. There's just too much of it. Way upstream from the lodge, where outlet streams form the Alagnak at a place called the Forks, the vastness of this land overwhelms. I've had the same feeling in the sub-Arctic region of northern Quebec and a bit of it in Yellowstone in the fall when the tourists are gone and you get away from the roads.

At the Forks the tundra runs on to the horizon, the famous Iliamna Region to the north. To the southwest, off in the distance, lies a low, ancient, volcanic ridge, beyond which is the Valley of Ten Thousand Smokes. Jack told me, almost reverently, that the predominant feature we could see was called Maggie's Nipple.

I went clear up to the Forks twice with Jack, a long run and certainly not necessary to catch fish. But we knew we'd see no other fishermen, which was the same as saying we'd see no other humans. I found it hard there to concentrate on the fishing. It's not often in a lifetime you get to places where there's only a very small chance that you will run across another human. There are places like that still, but not many.

❖

It was at the Forks that Jack hooked into a huge rainbow. It was the last week of the season and I didn't care if Jack fished as long as he was around. Like the other guides, he'd been working seven days a week because the season is so short. But I certainly didn't need him—or want him for that matter—at my shoulder every minute of the day, even though he wasn't supposed to fish. Just so long as he and the bear repellent were always handy.

The fish hit where the currents of the two rivers joined and it was instantly clear that Jack had his hands full. Because the current was heavy, there was no chasing this fish. Jack stood in the backwater near the bank between the two currents and tried not to get too far into his backing. The rainbow ripped out line and Jack pumped the fish back. A bald eagle landed in a dead tree fifty yards across the river as if to watch.

I stood on the bank opposite the eagle and watched. The big trout had the advantage of the heavy current, and Jack's rod—a standard six-weight trout rod—was under enormous strain. The tip snapped down and vibrated wildly every time the fish shook his head or ran. This went on for several minutes, and it was touch-and-go until the trout dashed across the main current into the gentler water of the left channel, and now it appeared that Jack had a chance.

He managed to get some line back on the reel, and from up on the bank I could finally see the huge, bright-colored slab of a fish. As the trout got close it shook its head and sprinted for deeper water and the heavier current. But Jack managed to stop it just short, got line back again, and worked the fish in close.

I stepped into the river about the same time Jack reached for the fish. As he knelt in the shallows there was some confusion and some spray flying around because you don't just grab a fish like this one. Jack knew that, of course, but I had a momentary vision of not getting to see the thing. A second later, though, he came up with the big trout cradled in one arm, trout and guide dripping wet.

Jack was grinning from ear to ear. I couldn't tell who was more excited, him or me. We admired the fish, took photos, and taped it, both length and girth. My guide was clearly thrilled and I was happy for him. Jack held the fish in the shallows over the clear, gravel bottom. As far as we knew, the trout was larger than any that had been caught during the week, but this rainbow would remain a private victory. The big trout swam slowly out of Jack's hands, turned, and disappeared into the darker, deeper water.

Jack stood and we shook hands. "I have to tell you, that made my whole season," he said.

That night at the lodge Jack calculated that the trout would have weighed nearly ten pounds. And he confessed that he had told a couple of the other guides, guys he could trust. Guys who could absolutely keep a secret. He was still beaming.

I sat on the veranda in front of the lodge dining room at twilight. The lodge sits on a bluff above a bend in the river and I had given the veranda a ten on the scale I use to rate cocktail porches. I was thinking about Jack's big trout, the more-than-respectable rainbows I had taken that day, and a bass I caught during our videotaping on the Lake of the Ozarks just days before.

I had been with Guido's son, Dion Hibdon, an up-and-coming bass pro in his own right. We had been using Dion's boat for wide shots, but the camera had been transferred to Guido's boat for some close work. During the break Dion said, "I'll throw to that side and you throw to this'n."

I picked up a spinning rod and discovered—of all things—that I was nervous as hell. Out of the corner of my eye I saw Guido flip a little jig about thirty feet into a water-level crack in the side of a boathouse. Guido Hibdon is to a lightweight spinning rod what Itzhak Perlman is to a violin.

Although he's only in his late forties, Guido is, in some ways, considered the patriarch of the bass circuit, and he has the beard, the grizzled look, and the experience to match. Like Brauer, he's won hundreds of thousands of dollars on the tour and has earned a bundle in endorsements. He's won scores of tournaments, including the BASS Masters Classic, which is the piscatorial equivalent of winning the Masters, or Wimbledon. It might even be harder. There are thousands of bass fishing clubs that hold sanctioned tournaments all over the country. Thus, there is a huge base of "semi-pro" anglers to feed the pro circuit, not unlike professional baseball. The competition is unbelievable. And yet, like any other sport, the truly great and skilled are in the money time and again.

Dion and I were one boathouse down from Guido and I was hoping I could just chuck my crankbait toward open water. But Dion had given me the boathouse and had zipped his Texas-rigged plastic worm toward the middle of the lake. So I kind of tossed one in toward the boathouse, just wanting to get respectably close. I also hoped Guido wasn't watching.

There was a school of shad off the left corner of the boathouse and an ominous dark shape just below them. I put my next cast over the milling shad, began to retrieve, and the dark shape gobbled my crankbait. The shad exploded in all directions and a nice little two-and-a-half-pound bass jumped clear out of the water. "Well, lookie there," said Dion quietly. And then he whistled at his father. Guido looked over and smiled and said, "There you go." I felt like I had just won the BASS Masters Classic.

❖

The sun was almost down and purple shadows were lengthening across the tundra. The Alagnak hissed quietly below the veranda on its way to the Bering Sea. Ken Taylor came by, cocktail in hand, and sat down in the chair next to me. Most people in camp called him "General" because indeed he was one, although he'd been retired for several years.

As a young Army Air Corps pilot stationed in the Hawaiian Islands on December 7, 1941, he was among the very few fighter pilots who managed to get aloft that day. He and a fellow pilot, George Welch, were credited with shooting down the first Japanese planes of World War II for our side. For more than five decades he and his former colleague kept the secret—who actually shot down the first one. They had decided not to reveal the truth until one of them died. Welch did die, and still Ken Taylor keeps the secret. Think about it.

We discovered that we shared a passion for good martinis, good storytelling, and good jokes. We became camp friends and this modest man insisted that I call him Ken. We fished with different guides during the day and got together in the evening to compare notes. He was an admirer of my guide, the affable Jack Davidson, and I was tempted to tell him about Jack's big trout but didn't have the chance. "You look lost in thought, my friend," he said in his soft Oklahoma accent as he made himself comfortable.

I admitted to have been thinking about my most recent plunge into the world of tournament bass fishermen, and the bass I'd caught under the nose of Guido Hibdon. He insisted I tell him the whole story, and he found it amusing that I had been intimidated.

In turn, he confessed—again—to having the same feeling about fly fishing. We had discussed this one night at dinner, and I had gone through the it's-simpler-than-it-looks routine and offered a lesson. So far, we hadn't gotten around to it.

A large fish had porpoised midstream several times and I was seriously considering a few casts off the lodge dock. I had a rod propped against the porch railing.

"I can see that fish is annoying you," the General said with a twinkle in his eye.

"If you'll guard my drink I'll go down and make a few casts," I said.

"The last time I had anything to do with guard duty I believe the Civil War was on, but I think I'm up to it. And for an extra one hundred dollars I won't tell passersby that you fish for bass." He was chuckling.

I walked out on the dock, stripped out line, and began casting where I thought I'd seen the fish roll. From up on the hill I heard, "Your drink's just fine, Jim. Everything is under control."

Someone passing in the gloom might have thought there was a madman on the dock, laughing alone there as rosy finches twittered in the brush. But a general was guarding my cocktail.

I made a couple of dozen casts, really just to be doing it more than anything. There was a distant burst of laughter from the club room and then it was quiet again. I heard the tinkle of the General's ice cubes. The river was narrow in front of the camp and as I halfheartedly covered the water I thought about the spectacle of fish that pass within easy casting distance of this dock during four short months. It is a pageant with roughly 4.5 million participants. Every second year when the humpys (pink salmon) are running you can add 2 million or 3 million more to the parade. In other words, 40,000 fish could pass by the dock during any given day. That's roughly 28 salmon per minute or about one-half fish every second. I stayed on the dock for about fifteen minutes, never seeing the fish that rolled, or making contact with any of the 419 others that might have cruised by during that time. I headed for the veranda.

In the dim light from the dining room window Ken pointed to my drink. "It's a little watery now, but there was nothing I could do about that since the jug is in your room."

But I congratulated him on a successful guard detail.

Just then a couple of fishermen and several of the guides, including Jack, came out onto the veranda.

"Well now, here's Jack," said the General. "How's Jack this evening?"

Jack said he was just fine and asked about the General's day.

"It was wonderful," the General replied. "But let me ask you something, Jack."

"Sure."

"Is it true that you caught a whopper today?"

Laughter rolled across the tundra.

14

TOM'S POOL

Greg Gerling and I were sitting at the kitchen table in a pleasant house in a copper mining town in northern Quebec where, quite unexpectedly, we were spending the night. We were just in from a salmon camp even farther north, and discovered that our plane wasn't going out until the next morning and the only hotel in town was full.

The hotel had an arrangement with several local families and we found ourselves staying with a French-Canadian couple who agreed to feed us and put us up for the night. The lady of the house whipped up a wonderful meal and her husband kept the wine and brandy handy. Best of all, they had two truly beautiful daughters who were with us for dinner and stayed around after the meal.

The family seldom got company from the outside, the little town being so far north that it was reachable only by air or rail. So Mom and Dad and the two beauties wanted to hear all about our trip. The daughters deluxe especially wanted to know what happened to Greg's wrist, which was black and blue and covered in bandages. Their father had fished for salmon and was thus interested in detail, so I was explaining how we had been sitting on a rock above a quiet little pool loaded with Atlantic salmon smolts. They were rising to a caddis hatch. Greg and I had been discussing the propriety of fishing for six-inch fish with nine-weight salmon rods—if we could find light-enough tippet material, let alone the right flies.

It was midafternoon and neither of us had raised a salmon all day. We'd seen fish roll, as they had been doing every day, so we knew salmon were there. But we couldn't pay a fish to take, and I was finally down to the weird stuff in some fly boxes that hadn't seen daylight in some time. We had the middle stretch of the camp's water—pools nine through sixteen—and we had pounded half of them with nary a smell.

We had started the day with ordinary Muddlers, a fly these George River salmon seemed to love. They liked a green version, tied by our friend and guide, Tom Black, even more. But Tom was out of green Muddlers and green tying material. So when we finally ran out of green Muddlers (a touch darker than kelly green) we switched to your basic brown version, and the salmon liked these too, especially riffle-hitched and skimmed on the surface. (Yes, there was a sniff of snootiness from one or two quarters in camp over the Muddler business, but that was about it.)

Every angler dreams about discovering a fly that consistently delivers the goods and, indeed, it looked for a time as though we had one, even though it was your plain old, everyday workhorse Muddler Minnow—a fly that has saved my ass more times than I can remember. But they seemed new and wonderful to the salmon, and Greg and I could do no wrong those first few days.

But today the mercurial Prince of the House of Salmonidae apparently wished to be appeased with a fly that did not yet exist. After hours of fruitless casting with Muddlers of all sizes, hitched, unhitched, floating, sinking, we had called up the reserves. We tried gaudy Durham Rangers, Silver Doctors, and Jock Scotts. We tried somber patterns like the Blue Charm, if you can call any traditional

Atlantic salmon fly somber. We tried big flies, small ones, single hooks, double hooks. We even went back to the General Practitioner, which originally was supposed to have been the hot ticket. The General Practitioner is a showy, nearly all orange fly that imitates shrimp, which, under normal circumstances, Atlantic salmon like as much as you and I do. Somehow Greg had gotten word that the General Practitioner was the big producer before we left for the river and had tied a bunch of them. In fact, he did not stop tying until he was pulling on his waders the first afternoon in camp. When we exited the airplane in Schefferville the cabin floor was littered with golden pheasant trimmings. But the George River salmon didn't like General Practitioners the first day, or any day.

So there we were, on our rock, watching salmon smolts (two- to four-year-old salmon) gorging on bugs, getting ready for their journey to Ungava Bay, where they would continue north until reaching the Hudson Strait. There they would swing east into the Labrador Sea, and finally out into the brooding North Atlantic. The lucky ones would be back to the George, some as grilse after just one year at sea, most of them as adult salmon with two or three years in the ocean and weighing twelve to fifteen pounds. But bigger salmon have been taken on the George, fish that have been at sea four years or more and return in the twenty-five-pound class. I was searching through some musty fly boxes examining patterns like the Skykomish Sunrise, an Umpqua Special, the notorious Skunk—a killer on my home coho and chinook rivers in Michigan. I didn't have a clue and set the box on the caribou moss and lit a cigar. Greg was lighting his pipe. "I've got an idea," he said as we hunched against the wind.

I was up for anything at that point.

"Just for the hell of it why don't you pick a fly from my stuff and I'll pick something from yours. Maybe it will change our luck."

So we exchanged fly boxes and, sure enough, I got a little excited as I scrutinized Gregory's inventory. He had tied a number of savory-looking patterns that I didn't have. From one of his fly boxes I chose a Green Butt. I had a couple of extra-large Muddlers with extremely dense, round heads (instead of tapered), but flat at the front. These had been tied on extended-shank #2 hooks by a friend who used them exclusively at night for big browns when he wasn't giving them to friends. He used prime, darkly mottled turkey feathers and his Muddlers were a work of art. Gerling had a gleam in his eye, sensing that they were special.

"Help yourself," I said. What better place for a beautiful fly from Michigan's north woods than the remote, sub-Arctic tundra region of northern Quebec, beautiful in its own way. And to be hurled at the comely Atlantic salmon no less? I was very pleased.

I asked Greg if he had used a Green Butt yet and he said no, so I was feeling a little smug as I knotted it to my leader. I was feeling luckier already, as though the salmon were out there saying, *That's what we've been waiting for! A Green Butt!*

Even though the Muddler Greg picked was bigger and more elegant than any Muddler we had used so far, I had my doubts. After all, these fish had been turning their noses up at Muddlers all day. "But not at a Muddler like this one," said Greg as he held the fly up and admired it. He had that feeling; I could see it on his face. And sometimes that's all it takes. When your confidence level is up I think you fish with more care. Your presentations are automatically better and that's half the game.

Greg tied on the big Muddler and headed up the pool; I headed down, admiring the Green Butt snug in my hook keeper, but with images of it snug in the corner of a big salmon's yap.

Across the river a pod of caribou sifted the wind, cautious about crossing, reacting to the signals that spanned the wide river, not knowing the strange, new scents. Behind them, up on the low hill in the distance were two forms, one nearly all white resting easily on its haunches, the other a salt-and-pepper mix lying on its belly. They were a vision of patience, these two huge Arctic wolves. The caribou were migrating and were everywhere on the tundra. The wolves often waited by the river, hoping to ambush a young or old caribou as it climbed from the water, tired from the swim across. The wolves shadowed the caribou in their march across the tundra, bringing them down only infrequently and with great difficulty and danger to themselves. The two wolves on the hill watched the caribou and for a few moments I watched the wolves, much too far away for my satisfaction. I wanted to be over there, sitting next to them, even more than I wanted right then to catch a salmon.

We were fishing from the bank, which is basically the drill on the George, although some prefer to fish from the big freighter canoes. The river is wide and for the most part too deep to wade. There are spots where you can wade, but most of the pools are against the banks, which makes for very pleasant fishing.

At the lower end of the pool I worked out line and began covering the water, the #8 Green Butt looking good to me, at least, as I stripped it in with short, steady jerks. The action began at once as a vicious mob of six-inch Atlantic salmon pounced on the fly. It wasn't pretty. I moved on, trying to remember a long-ago military class on crowd control, flipping little salmon out of the water, one after another.

I began lengthening my casts, hoping to out-distance the eager little bandits. I marveled that somewhere along the way they make the transition from unsuspecting pint-size tyrants to unpredictable ghosts, at times so wary and difficult that some anglers give up the sport suspecting they are the creative product of various writers' imaginations. But right then I could say that I had caught a dozen

Atlantic salmon on a dozen successive casts, which I was certain would make a great saloon story. It was then that I looked upstream and saw Greg coming down the bank.

"We've got a problem here," he said, holding out his right arm.

There, buried in his wrist, was the big Muddler.

❖

Up to that point it had been one of those escapades that come our way just often enough to keep the flame burning bright. We had caught salmon after salmon, mostly on Muddlers despite the array of lovely traditionals we had with us. One day Greg caught three fish during our lunch break, practically with sandwich in hand. One was a big hook-billed male that ran him a couple hundred yards down the river. Nearly all the fish were taking on or near the surface, were fresh from the sea, and jumped like scalded cats.

It seemed like every time you saw an obvious lie there was an salmon there. And better still, one willing to take. The days were sunny and we fished in our shirtsleeves. Our guide, Tom Black, was an old friend who had been fishing the river since the age of eleven. His Dad, Lou, also an old friend, was in camp—an Atlantic salmon crazy who has chased these fish all over the world. We had fish, we had friends, we had good weather. If you don't thank the Fish Gods when it all comes together like this, you're either crazy or truly spoiled.

On the day Greg caught his three salmon at lunchtime, I had been fishless. Actually, I had three fish on that morning, but all three had thrown the hook. We were on the lower pools, way down river from camp, and when we started back late in the afternoon it looked as though I might be in for a fishless day. There was hope though. Unlike the other sports, Greg, Lou, Tom, and I fished every evening in the camp pools after dinner. Louie had been fishing the George for nearly two decades—three to four weeks every year—and knew it better than the guides. So most evenings we took fish. But Tom wasn't going to wait until after dinner. "I've got a little pool on the side of the big rapids we'll try on the way back. It's a one rod pool. You'll have twenty minutes, maybe a half-hour, and we can still make dinner."

Halfway up the rapids, running the bank most of the way, Tom put us ashore below a huge rock that was maybe half the size of a one-car garage. The rock was part of the shoreline, but extended perhaps twenty-five feet out into the river. We walked up the bank and around the rock, keeping back from the water. There, on the upstream side of this outsized boulder, was a gorgeous little pool. It was deep and clear and smooth as glass. Just beyond it, the rapids zipped past.

"This is kind of a private spot," Tom said. "None of the other guides ever fish it, but it's been real sweet to me."

That polished surface begged for a dry fly and I tied on a parachute Adams. Tom stood next to me and explained the deal. "Start the fly out about fifteen feet off the bank near the top of the pool and mend line immediately. Let the fly float right down to the base of the rock. Do that a half-dozen times and if nothing happens lengthen your cast a couple of feet and do it all over again. If you get out to the far side and still nothing, we'll go home."

Our side of the rock—the upstream side—was almost flat and nearly vertical, rising about fifteen feet above the water. The back side was a gradual slope. Out of the corner of my eye I saw Greg climb the rock, lie down on its top, and inch forward until he was peeking over the upstream edge.

The parachute Adams (one of the deadliest flies ever invented, lethal in any size, anywhere on the planet) was tied on a #6, lightwire hook. When I got it on the water it looked like a little lighthouse out there with its bright white upright wing flashing in the sunlight.

At first I had a hell of a time keeping the fly from dragging because there was almost no current against the bank. There was very little current in the pool at all, but as I worked the fly out I had more line to work with and mending was easier. Out toward the center there was just enough current…to…move…the…fly…about…this…fast. If I threw a big loop right away I began getting drag-free floats, but couldn't maintain them all the way down to the rock wall at the base of the pool. Staying back from the water's edge didn't help either.

On what might have been my tenth cast I heard a melodramatic gasp from the top of the rock. "Did you see that!" Greg whispered.

I hadn't seen anything and shook my head.

"Let the fly swing all the way down before you pick up and then do it real easy. A big fish came up and looked and then went back down again." He was still whispering, like a golf announcer.

I managed to get the fly back to about the same place, mended as much line as I could, and watched as the fly drifted lazily down the pool. This time I saw it just as Greg whispered, "There he is!" I swear I saw Gerling hunch down even farther beyond the rim of the rock.

I saw the big shape materialize. The salmon was nearly vertical just inches under the fly, its body extended and facing upstream, drifting backward with the current. For perhaps four or five seconds it stayed with the fly, still just barely beneath it. I could actually see its right eye staring at the Adams.

And then suddenly it was gone. I discovered I was leaning forward with my casting arm extended as far as I could reach. I nearly fell over.

"You're still getting a little drag right at the end of your float," Greg said.

I sensed Tom easing in behind me. "Put it down as gently as you can," he said.

I dried the fly with a few false casts and put it back out. It landed pretty softly—I thought—and again I mended all the line I could. Once again the little fly began its journey down the length of that deep, dark pool. And once again the big salmon came from the shadows. I could see it now, four or five feet down, rising slowly until it stopped an inch from the fly. It drifted with the fly, watching it, for ten feet, not moving a muscle that I could see, and finally vanished again.

"That one was perfect!" said my spy from up on his perch.

It seemed to me that everything was happening in slow motion. Twice more the big fish came from the depths of the pool to intercept the fly. Twice more it drifted with it, not more than a gillplate away. Like most rational anglers (if there is such a thing) I know that fish do not think. Still, as I watched the fish examine the fly—scrutinize really—I couldn't help but wonder what was going on in the salmon's mind. What did it think it was seeing? What made it come time after time to inspect this tiny thing floating above it that bore no resemblance to anything it had been recently eating?

Once again the fly landed on the water and just as I was beginning to wonder how many times we'd repeat this majestic scene, the salmon again came to the fly and began its maddening drift backwards.

"If it doesn't take this time we'll change the pattern," I heard Tom say. Three feet, four feet, five feet—the fly and the salmon drifted as if one. And then there was just the slightest movement of its tail and a big snout broke the water, mouth agape, and gently rolled over on the fly. I remembered to say *Atlantic salmon* silently to myself and pulled the trigger.

The rest was anything but slow motion. The fish was out of the pool in a heartbeat and into the edge of the rapids. Somehow we got the fly line over the boulder and I chased the fish down the rocky shoreline, mindful of the lightwire hook. I managed to keep the fish out of the heavier current and it gave us three spectacular jumps at the edge of the seam. The hook held, and about twenty minutes later I waded out a few feet to be in the water as the salmon came in. I stumbled, fell, got wet, fractured the little finger on my left hand (as it turned out), but held on to the fish. Just then Lou came ashore in his canoe. He'd watched the whole thing from out in the river, holding in the current. For some reason we netted this salmon instead of tailing it, but there it was, a bright henfish of thirteen pounds.

That evening I declined to go out with the after-dinner salmon crew, and instead hiked across the tundra to a small, nameless tributary that entered the George upstream from camp. It was full of brook trout—or "specs" as they call them in Canada. I wanted to be alone. I wanted to let the drama of the afternoon simmer.

As darkness fell I wandered back to camp, where sundowners were being poured. It was a clear night, as most of them had been, and the whole crew was anticipating the spectacular, nightly display of the northern lights. But my mind was still on the afternoon's matinee: Greg hunkered on top of his granite outpost, spying as carefully as a schoolboy sneaking a peek through the neighbor girl's window; Tom sucking in his breath each time the fly began its little trip down the pool; and the phantom that came again and again and turned out not to be a phantom after all.

❖

So I showed the girls, by holding my fingers apart, just how big the hook was that got stuck in Greg's wrist. They were wide-eyed. And hanging on our every word. And I noticed that Dad was beginning to give them—and us—the eye. Now Greg was showing them how it had gone into his wrist, way past the barb. The two beauties gasped.

"A gust of wind caught the fly line," Greg explained.

Like the elegant salmon that had come to my dry fly, the details of Greg's little problem were still fresh in my mind. I had asked him what he wanted to do. He wanted to know if I had ever done the string method of extracting a hook. I never had, but I'd done a few of the push-the-point-through-and-clip-off-the-barb deals. But I'd read about the string method and seen a step-by-step illustration.

"I've never done it either, but it's supposed to be the new, easier way, and this sucker has to come out, so let's do it."

Using some heavy tippet material, we tried the so-called string method, Greg mostly calling the shots. "When I say go you pull quick and smooth."

He said go and I pulled. He should have gotten a medal for not screaming when that big hook did not come out and he went straight up into the air and his wrist started to swell and turn blue. Neither of us knew what went wrong, but I could barely stand to watch him while he hobbled around, holding his arm. But he was a tough cookie, an ex-Marine and a big-city fireman. Finally he said "We're not doing that again." I knew I wasn't.

I suggested we find Tom and have a consultation. Because our guide was also a longtime friend, neither of us cared if he napped or fished when things were slow. We just wanted him close in case we needed the canoe to chase a fish. We found him sound asleep on his back in a clump of blueberry bushes. Every blueberry in an arm's-length circle around him had been eaten. We woke Tom, who burped as we pointed to Greg's wrist. "Oh my, that will never do," said Tom.

So we decided that Greg would lie down, Tom would sit on him, I'd kneel on his arm and try to get the hook out the conventional way.

"Whatever you do, once you start, don't stop for anything. Keep going until you get it out," Greg said. His wrist looked terrible and I felt like hell.

Tom sat on him, I put a knee on his arm, and finally managed to get the point and barb back up through the skin. I clipped the point and barb off with my needlenose sidecutters and the big hook slipped right out. Greg walked down to the river and rinsed his wrist. When he came back Tom said, "What do you want to do now?"

"What the hell, let's fish," said Greg.

Our Canadian friends enjoyed the tale but Dad was not long in dismissing the girls, rather pointedly I thought. As the girls left the kitchen there were winks and smiles flying all over the place.

Greg and I went out for a while, down the street to a bar, had a few beers, and walked back to the house. "What do you think?" he asked. "Will they be waiting for us?"

It was Dad who was waiting for us. He was most cordial, closed the front door behind us, and followed us upstairs to our second-story bedroom wanting to know if we needed anything.

Sometime during the night I had to get rid of some beer. I stood in the dark, fumbling with the bedroom door. I couldn't get it open even though the doorknob turned easily enough. Now Greg was awake. So I turned on the light. Still I couldn't get the door open. Greg got out of bed and tried. As a fireman, he figured it out. "We're bolted in from the outside!" We both started to laugh.

Finally I said that locked in or not, I still had to piss. Even as I was saying it, Greg was sliding open the bedroom window and popping the screen. I turned out the lights and we took turns wetting down our host's roof.

Still amazed at our prisonerlike status, we talked in the dark across the room half hoping for a discreet tap-tap on the door, but mostly doing a replay. Greg remembered his three lunchtime salmon, and I saw again the bright henfish coming up out of that deep little pool. "I wonder if that spot has a name?"

"Don't you know? It's called Tom's Pool," he said.

15

❖

Hallelujah Chorus

The back of the vehicle opens and two furry little noses pop over the tailgate, black buttons in the air, sifting the wind even as they jump to the ground. For five minutes there is a free-for-all as the pup piles onto the annoyed older dog, trying to play, not yet aware of the program.

The shotgun is loaded and the merry little band sets off across a stubble field toward a distant woodlot full of slash and briars. The veteran beagle is already all business, nose to the bare, hard ground searching for signs of Mr. Cottontail. The pup is beginning to remember former lessons.

It is nearly the end of rabbit season and there are patches of snow still in the big cornfield. It is crisp, but not especially cold, and the sky is blue. The days are longer and already there have been hints of what's to come.

The entourage gains the woodlot and the dogs disappear into the briars. My command post is a nice flat stump near the center. I double-check the safety on the shotgun, climb up, and light a cigar. Above the briars now, I can follow the dogs by watching the brush ripple.

There is a patch of snow at the base of the stump. Sunlight, coming through the bare limbs of the oaks, is melting the edge, creating a miniature runoff—a single, tiny, liquid diamond every minute or so. The clock is ticking. A fox squirrel chirrs, uneasy as he discovers three unwelcome visitors in his woodlot. A soft little breeze brings with it that ever-so-faint but unmistakable earth scent: that hint of promise that fills the soul. At the base of my stump the tempo increases. The clock is ticking.

❖

It was a glorious June day and three fish were feeding in a gentle chute at the head of a small island. I hurried through the knee-deep water to get within casting range. Downstream I heard my father whistle. I turned to see him fast to a fish. I waded across the river into the shallows and raced downstream. I came up behind him just as he reached down, got his hand around the fish, and lifted it glistening and dripping from the water.

"What do you suppose it is, a brown trout or a brook trout?" he wondered aloud.

After careers involving Lake Erie perch we were astonished at the gaudy colors of the sleek fish. My father removed the fly and released the trout and we both knew that perch were forever in our past. "Wow, that was something!" he said.

The trout had taken one of the little yellow dry flies the guy in the shop had sold us. "This is what they want," he had promised. It was my father's first trout, and later we would learn that the fly it took was called a Sulphur Dun. My father would fish dry flies almost exclusively until the end of his life. The main branch of the Au Sable River in the northern Lower Peninsula of Michigan would become his home river, and he rarely strayed.

Back upstream, I was excited to discover that several trout were now feeding in the run by the island. I stripped out line, made a few clumsy false casts, and put the Sulphur pattern a lucky foot above the first fish. The bright little fly tumbled along on the clear water looking like a kernel of buttered popcorn in the sunlight. The second trout obligingly took it and changed my life forever. It was my turn to whistle but my father was already heading upstream. The fish raced about the deep pool below the chute, but minutes later we were admiring the trout, its golden hue marked with black and red spots. "This must be a brown," I said as I admired *my* first trout.

"Then the one I caught must have been a brook trout," my father replied.

At that moment the Au Sable also became my home river, but unlike my father I would wander far and wide. One trout stream was not enough for me.

Neither of us caught another trout that weekend and we fished hard. It was as though the trout gods were saying *You each get one look and then you start paying your dues.*

Nearly two decades later my father bought a handsome cabin on a scenic bend on the river and became a fixture in that stretch. You can bet your last dollar that over the years he paid his dues. So there wasn't much that escaped his attention in the home pools. He had a favorite spot he called the "brook hole" (as in "brookie") upstream at the first bend, and it was a rare day he couldn't get the attention of at least one of its residents, always with a dry fly. He loved the game.

❖

From the near corner of the woodlot there suddenly comes a tentative yip, then another. And then Katy is in full cry. A moment later Sarah joins in with her unpolished squalling. My hackles rise as they always do at the first notes of this primeval song, this music of prehistory that has somehow managed to survive generations of dogs named Muffy that can't find their way to the back door. The skirmish moves east and the battle cries of my little troopers fade a bit. I remain patiently, silently, on my stump.

❖

It was a cold, sleety day on the Firehole when, out of the mist of a hot spring, I was startled to see a fly line emerge; a backcast unrolling in a slow, picture-perfect loop, the stark white fly line straightening, hanging in the air, then disappearing again into the gray. I stopped on the bank, fascinated, and watched. Not a sound came from within that miniature fog bank. A moment later the fly line emerged again, the loop even tighter this time. At the precise moment the line was fully extended, it began its forward journey and once again disappeared into the mist. I watched for several minutes. It was the most beautiful casting I had ever seen, at least the backcasts were. Then it stopped. I thought I heard a match being struck. Nothing happened. I continued on my way. I hiked along the bank toward the stretch of the river I wanted. I looked back and there it was again, the white line unfurling from the gray, hanging over the river, above the valley, underscoring the distant mountains. And once again it disappeared.

The rabbit is sticking to the edge of the woodlot, moving slowly, unconcerned about the dogs, which are well behind. The dogs almost never run fast unless there's a momentary sighting of the rabbit, which is rare. Even then, it would be the pup that would dash forward. Katy might let out an excited bawl, but would keep her nose to the ground, working exclusively on scent, not sight, the mark of a good rabbit dog. Who knows what tricks Mr. Cottontail might play?

The dogs move at a brisk, workmanlike pace. The woodlot rings with beagle music.

I pulled on the hip boots, took another look at the map, and locked the truck. I checked the compass, sighted on a red pine near the crest of a distant ridge, and, with fly rod in hand, started out.

Twenty minutes later I reached the top of the first ridge. The map said I had one more to go. I took another sighting and set off again.

On the map the little blue squiggle was about an inch long. Every blue squiggle I see on maps of trout country, especially those with no name, excites me. It might be nothing more than a cedar-choked rivulet, and often is. Then again, it might be something else.

A pair of grouse thundered up just ahead. I was at the base of the second ridge and climbing. I had a good feeling. At the crest, the ridge was broad and I pushed my way through a stand of aspen. And there it was.

The little stream was about four feet wide, twisting through a small, open valley. I knew that it fed a famous trout stream some distance away, but entered the big river as a mere trickle, giving no sign of this upstream surprise. The valley was surrounded by stands of aspen with a few pines here and there. At every bend in the creek there was a dark pool swirling against the bank.

The meadow was alive with hoppers. Above the first pool I tied on a hopper pattern. The fly landed near the bank, twisted in the current, and floated out of the pool. I made several more casts and nothing happened. I caught my backcast on some brush, retrieved it, and moved to the next pool.

I made three or four casts, and nothing. I couldn't believe this gorgeous little piece of hidden water didn't have trout. My hopper pattern was a big one and I replaced it with another that was smaller and plainer.

The fly landed in the heart of the pool, a few feet below the spot I was aiming for. It disappeared with a splash. I saw a couple of flashes in the water. A minute later I brought a ten-inch brook trout flopping onto the bank. It was darker than its big-river cousins, the white slashes on its fins bright in the sunlight.

All afternoon I moved from pool to pool. The little stream, in its tucked-away valley, became my private playground. Over the years it's been the place I go when the possibility of seeing a fisherman during the course of a day is more than I can handle. I can still see that small hopper pattern landing on the water again and again that first day, skittering in the sunlight at every bend, disappearing in a bright flash. I caught a trout in nearly every pool, beautiful little brookies that I was beginning to suspect had never seen a fly.

It is a small valley, almost too small to be called one. It's more like a glen tucked away between two ridges. The fishable stretch of the brook is not more than a hundred yards as the crow flies. But it's a fairyland just the same.

The rabbit hangs a sharp left and cuts right through the center of the woodlot, into the thickest briars. I know that Mr. Cottontail is becoming unnerved by the methodical pursuit of the two dogs. It might be time for a trick. Katy and Sarah, on the other hand, are deliriously happy. They're still in full cry and I can even hear their tails whacking the brush as they go. Nothing like a hot bunny trail. I'm happy, too. Happy to be outside with my dogs, basking in the ever-warming sunlight, and knowing that opening day is right around the corner and not a distant dream. I notice that Sarah's voice seems to be smoothing a bit. But I'm full of memories.

The Fin-Nor barely hummed as the salmon peeled out the fly line and nearly all of my backing. Unless you're a poacher, that's the only problem with the Fin-Nor. It doesn't make music while it's working. I was stuck on a submerged rock fifty yards from shore just above a rapids. The rock was tilting precariously and I was on the verge of going down the river, perhaps even to the bottom of the river.

Earlier, with the sun, I had worked my way out into the George by going from one submerged rock to another. The George River is huge there and I could see salmon rolling far from shore. Like a fool, I followed a zigzag course of boulders farther and farther from shore, but closer and closer to the Holy Grail.

Eventually I was chest-deep in water and could go no farther. I began casting, blindly covering the water with a big, green Muddler. Suddenly the line stopped and straightened and I instinctively set the hook. A salmon somersaulted far out in the river and we were off to the races. At least the salmon was.

It was imperative that I get back on shore, and the moment I turned I realized I was in a fix. A gray cover of clouds hung above the tundra and the sun was gone. So, too, was my rocky trail back to dry land.

Our guide had taken Greg upriver to the next set of pools. Alone there, that river suddenly looked even bigger, those rapids just below me even wilder. But my backing was almost down to the arbor on the reel.

I stepped off my rock back in the direction I thought I'd come from, probing with my foot, and landed on a rock about half the size of a desk. For a second I thought I had it made, then the rock tilted to the downstream side. I just barely had any footing on the slanting rock; in fact, I was slowly slipping off. Water began trickling over the tops of my waders. I still held the rod, but I had completely forgotten about it and the salmon.

I got one arm out of my vest—I was simply going to drop that. I still didn't realize I was holding the rod. I knew I was going off any moment and I was trying like hell to figure out if I should try to get out of my waders.

About then, like the just-in-time arrival of the cavalry, I heard an outboard. I thought it might be Tom, but it turned out to be his father. Lou came chugging up through the rapids in the big freighter canoe. I was well beyond feeling foolish, and yelled my bloody head off. I thought for sure Lou was going to go on by, but at the last moment I saw the canoe turn and then come at me with a burst of speed.

I was now nearly up to my neck in water. Lou could see I was about to go, so there wasn't any time for adroit boat handling. And he couldn't slow much anyway or the current would carry him into the rapids sideways. He barely cut his speed as he reached me. I lost my footing and was swept off the rock, but not before I got one arm over the side of that canoe. Louie gunned the engine. I thought for a second the canoe was going to tip. My legs were dragged under, back toward the outboard. The only thing out of the water was my face and left arm.

Lou aimed for shore and yelled "Keep your tip up!" It was then that I realized I still had the rod, clutched tightly to my chest.

I stuck the rod straight up in the air, the cream-colored fly line sailing over Lou's shoulder. I knew I couldn't possibly have the fish.

Less than a minute later my butt was dragging on the bottom and the canoe grated on shore as Lou killed the engine.

I sat there in a few inches of water, only a partial basket case, and started to thank Lou.

"Don't worry about it. Just get up and get your fish in," he said.

A joke, of course. But I managed to stand and discovered the fly line still attached to something well upriver. Soaking wet, I started up the bank and began to get backing on the reel. Lou followed and we finally caught up with the fish.

"I think it's a small salmon," Lou said. "And it's probably whipped from towing that fly line and backing all over hell and gone."

Moments later, we had the fish on shore. It was a small Atlantic salmon, about eight pounds. It was a lovely fish, but certainly not worth dying for. I slipped the fly out and held the salmon in the shallows until it swam slowly away.

A pod of caribou crossed the river, swimming easily through the base of the rapids. I wondered.

❖

The song of the hounds changes suddenly. It goes from long, smooth, medium-pitched notes to intermittent high-pitched yips. I know that the rabbit has played a trick of some kind. Then the dogs are silent. They're working out the puzzle. I see a movement in the brush. Here comes the rabbit, moving slowly, quite unconcerned. Listening for the dogs, the rabbit is unaware of the hunter, who stands still as a heron.

❖

The old riverboat lay in the woods, full of dirt, leaves, and water. The rusty trailer was nearby. The trailer had spoked wheels from a 1938 Ford, complete with the original V-8 hubcaps. The tires were bald. By the end of that April day the boat had been cleaned and sat on sawhorses at the river house, just yards away from the river that had been its home for forty-eight years.

The boat is twenty-four feet long and thirty-eight inches wide. The V-bow and the less-tapered stern slope up at graceful angles. The bottom is flat. A few feet behind the bow there is a swivel seat for the fisherman. The seat sits on top of a three-compartment structure that is an integral part of the boat. On either side of the seat are two storage compartments. Directly beneath the seat is a livewell. The compartment is sealed off and has five holes in the bottom to let river water in. A rectangular hole in the front of the compartment, just below the angler's seat, allows the sport to slip his trout literally between his legs—plop!—right into the livewell. The seat is mounted on the lid to the compartment and, at float's end, it can be removed to gain access to the livewell. These days the livewell serves mostly as a beer cooler. Below the gunwales, inside, are pegs for holding fly rods. At the stern is another seat for the guide.

The speed of the boat is regulated by a short length of chain that trails the boat. The chain is attached to a rope that is tied to an eyehook on the stern. Most riverboat owners have two or three chains of various weights and lengths to control the boat in different currents. These are rigged on separate ropes and are kept within reach on the floor near the stern seat. It's a simple matter, then, to reach back, grab the rope that's out, pull in the chain, and slip another over the side.

The riverboat is maneuvered with a pushpole. The operator essentially "steers" the boat by moving the stern to where he eventually wants the bow to be. The trick is to know what the boat will do in various currents and to pay attention to what the bow is doing twenty-four feet in front of you. In really slow water you run with no chains and use an oversize paddle to control the boat. The boat will run in just inches of water.

These boats are indigenous to the Au Sable and Manistee Rivers in the northern region of Michigan's Lower Peninsula. They are found nowhere else. There are only a few craftsmen building them today. They are an unbelievably wonderful way to fish dry flies. If the person running the boat knows what he's doing, drag-free floats of a hundred feet aren't uncommon.

As I mentioned in an earlier chapter, a neighbor kid owned the boat but hadn't used it in years. Three of us made him a deal he couldn't refuse. My brother-in-law, Ron Randlett, and I sacrificed a lot of fishing hours that summer to restore the queen to her former majesty. It took a month's worth of weekends just to get her stripped down to her earliest paint job. But by the end of the summer she was once again resplendent. So was the trailer, all repainted and rewired, the 1938 Ford V-8 hubcaps gleaming. We had the bottom of the boat fiberglassed, and on the day of her recommissioning voyage we installed a small brass plaque on the lid of the right-side storage compartment: 1941.

There must be by now a thousand fish stories connected with this elegant boat, just in the time we've owned her. Every voyage makes memories. The best so far, for me, was the day my son Jeff, in the front seat and throwing a pretty good loop for a ten-year-old, dropped the bumblebee pattern upstream from a log. The boat kept pace as the big black-and-yellow fly floated in the current. It reached the log and, right on cue, disappeared in a splashy rise. Moments later, with help from his Uncle Ron, we were admiring Jeff's first trout on a dry fly. An hour later we would float right past the island where Jeff's father and grandfather caught their first Au Sable trout twenty years before.

We keep the boat in the garage at the river house, where sometimes at night Ronnie and I will go out and putter with it, maybe give an errant dusty spot a swipe. Sometimes I just stare at it there in the dim light, its long, clean lines resting quietly on the old trailer. I wish it could speak to me. I want to hear the stories of fifty years ago, of the fishermen who cast their flies on the historic Au Sable from her bow, of the great trout that were lifted over her sides.

If it is possible to love an object, an inanimate thing, then I love that boat. More than any painting, more than any book, more than any fly rod, that comely lady owns a piece of my heart.

❖

The rabbit stops, sits up, and looks back, checking on the dogs. He has indeed played a trick on them in the thickest part of his briar patch. I can hear the dogs snuffling and snorting. Katy, I know, will figure it out as she always does. Rabbit trails crisscross the woodlot, many of them near my stump, which is one of the reasons I chose it for my command post. Cottontail rabbits, unlike snowshoes or jack rabbits, generally stick to a smallish territory and will stay in it unless they're pursued by big, fast dogs, which Katy and Sarah are not. They're dainty little worker-bees, my Katy and Sarah.

Suddenly Katy breaks into full cry. The puzzle is solved! Sarah joins in. The rabbit wiggles his big ears and lopes down the trail. I might let him pass by a couple of times. The dogs are having too much fun, even if they don't know it. Or maybe it's me having the fun. Five minutes go by and here come my troopers! They're bawling as loud as they can, tails threshing with excitement! Katy gives me a quick look. I make it out to be her thanks-for-nothing expression. (She tends toward business.) For an instant I'm embarrassed. Caught up in the excitement, however, I want to yell *Go team go!* but don't dare. Mr. Cottontail would then know the dark secret.

❖

The river was only inches deep, the water running over clean gravel. But there were channels and pools all around. It was late afternoon and trout were rising everywhere: above me, below me, on both sides of me. I was at the head of an island and just below one of the few deep pools on the main branch of the Au Sable. A cabin sat on the bluff on the north side. A rope swing hung from a branch above the river over one of the small pools. Two trout were rising below it.

Black caddis had been coming off steadily for over an hour. Without moving more than a few feet I'd caught nearly a dozen and a half trout—browns, brookies, and a rainbow. I fished to what I thought were larger trout, first to one side of the river and then to the other. Above, then below. I took a nice brown, about fourteen inches, hard against the island. The little six-and-a-half-foot Cortland bamboo fly rod was working hard. Upstream I took another brown at the base of the deeper pool. For two hours I caught trout after trout on that warm summer evening, releasing them at my feet, watching them zip away over the gravel. I lost count. Thirty? Was that possible? The trout gods do not give us such days very often.

Magically, the rings never stopped. But I did. I lit a cigar and simply watched. A mink hunted along the bank. A kingfisher chattered downstream. Trout rose everywhere.

❖

What's this! Katy, bawling at the top of her lungs, is off in one direction and Sarah, also in full cry, is off in another! My platoon has divided. While running the first rabbit, they came across the trail of a second. At least I hope it's two rabbits. With Sarah, you can't be certain. Squirrels, pheasants, and even mice have been known to distract her. Katy would run right over that greatest of temptations, Mr. Cock Pheasant, in order to keep on the trail of Mr. Cottontail.

The sun is higher. The smell of spring is clearly in the air. I take off the heavy hunting coat and hang it on the sapling next to my stump. The sapling is already showing a few tentative buds. Off in the distance a man and a small boy carry something into a bright, new barn, built the summer before.

A church bell peals, adding its notes to the beagle music that resounds throughout the woodlot. No matter how many times I've heard this symphony, it never fails to touch some corner of my soul. How do you explain how your hackles rise when those first notes pound skyward? How do you explain that your hallelujah chorus is a couple of beagles singing their ancient song, the notes sailing in the cool, clean air; reverberating through a bare-limbed woodlot; echoing across the countryside for a mile and in your head forever?

How?

How do you explain that your hallelujah chorus is the sound of large trout feeding on a lonely creek at midnight, each savage splash sending a charge of electricity up your spine, right through the top of your skull?

How?